Big World, Little World

A Green Anthology of Poetry and Prose

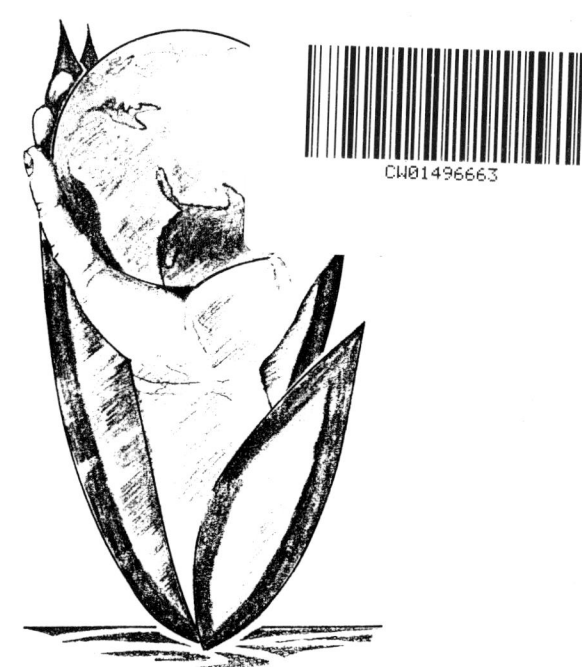

Compiled by Sue Stewart

Nelson

First edition 1991

Published by Thomas Nelson and Sons Ltd
Nelson House   Mayfield Road
Walton-on-Thames   Surrey
KT12 5PL   UK

51 York Place
Edinburgh
EH1 3JD   UK

Thomas Nelson (Hong Kong) Ltd
Toppan Building 10/F
22A Westlands Road
Quarry Bay   Hong Kong

Thomas Nelson Australia
102 Dodds Street
South Melbourne
Victoria 3205 Australia

Nelson Canada
1120 Birchmount Road
Scarborough   Ontario
M1K 5G4   Canada

Printed in Hong Kong

ISBN 0-17-401002-8
NPN 9 8 7 6 5 4 3 2 1

Contents

Songs of the Wild

Poems with an obvious 'song' (rhythm, rhyme, chant, repetition, onomatopoeia) and other literary forms

Airwaves

Things that fly and the air they fly in

What time is it?

Seasons, memories, forecasts and histories

Big World, Little World

Countries/planets/the world

Introduction

The world is ours, to enjoy and take care of. If it gets too sick, or too polluted, we won't be able to live healthy lives, eating the food we want to eat, breathing the air we want to breathe. It's part of us, and we are part of it.

Even the everyday expressions we use show how much we are a part of nature: we say someone has a sunny outlook, or is feeling under the weather. Faces can cloud over, tempers erupt, people turn over a new leaf. We have puppy love, mother hens and bear hugs. We can have a memory like an elephant or be as scared as a mouse. We talk of butterfly minds, budding talents.

These expressions are popular because they ring true: we are as much in keeping with the natural world as the seasons, plants or animals. So, before the world gets as sick as a parrot, let's be wise old owls. Each one of us can do something practical to help, from planting a tree to recycling a bottle. And by writing your own poems, stories and letters, you can reach lots of different people, even changing their minds or the way they think about the world.

Now THAT's magic!

Sue Stewart

Our School Went Green This Week

Our school went green this week.

Monday it was the walls
like grass five metres high;
Tuesday it was the ceilings,
like a green cloudless sky.

Our school went green this week.

Wednesday it was the water,
green as lemon and lime.
Thursday it was the yard:
a pool-table playtime.

Our school went green this week.

Friday it was the teachers
dripping all over the floor;
drops of bright green paint
from a man in the corridor.

Our school went green this week.

It was the caretaker, you see;
I don't think he quite understood
our green assembly.
Our school's being cleaned next week.

Martyn Wiley and Ian McMillan

The world's a paintbox

My childhood was spent on Hampstead Heath, a small patch of semi-natural green in the middle of London. It's small in real terms, no more than a couple of hundred acres. But through the eyes of an eight-year-old boy, it was absolutely huge; indeed, much too large to be properly encompassed at ground level. So my first relationship with trees started predictably: God had obviously put them on Earth for me to climb. And given my immersion in a competitive culture, it wasn't enough first to climb trees: I had to climb the very *highest* trees. I first learned about nature and my interdependence with nature, hanging precariously out of the branches of these wonderful, long-suffering trees, taking equal pleasure in the sense of danger, the sense of isolation and the sense of being utterly at home. From that time on I was completely hooked and I remain an unreconstructed dendrophile to this day. Which is why President Reagan's comment, 'Seen one tree, seen 'em all' doesn't really strike home with me!

from *Jonathon Porritt's Schumacher Lecture, 1988*

Flowers

I have never learnt the names of flowers.
From beginning, my world has been a place
Of pot-holed streets where thick, sluggish gutters race
In slow time, away from garbage heaps and sewers
Past blanched old houses around which cowers
Stagnant earth. There, scarce green thing grew to chase
The dull-grey squalor of sick dust; no trace
Of plant save few sparse weeds; just these, no flowers.

One day they cleared a space and made a park
There in the city's slums; and suddenly
Came stark glory like lightning in the dark,
While perfume and bright petals thundered slowly.
I learnt no names, but hue, shape and scent mark
My mind, even now, with symbols holy.

Dennis Craig

The Buttercup Experiment

From the overgrown lawn I plucked a buttercup
and held it under my sister's chin.
'This is the buttercup experiment,' I said,
'let's see if it shines yellow on your skin.'

It did. 'It means you like butter.'
We gathered more buttercups. The day was hot.
On the kitchen windowsill we arranged them
in a plastic beaker and a yoghurt pot.

How they glowed ..... like little suns,
or butter on toast, or flame of candlelight.
So much brighter than lemon, the dullness of mustard,
or the moon's pale face on a dark winter's night.

Wes Magee

Leaves were fluttering down all over the lawn, and because there had been a frost the night before the grass was all crunchy with white frost crystals.

As Tim pedalled about, he began catching the leaves when they floated near him, and putting them in the basket of his tricycle. He caught a red leaf, a yellow leaf, a brown leaf, a pale green leaf, a dark green leaf, and a silvery leaf. Then he caught another red leaf, two more brown leaves, and two more yellow leaves. Then he caught a great green leaf, the shape of a hand. Presently his basket was almost filled up with leaves. He pedalled back to the pond and showed all his leaves to the snails and the stone goblin.

'Look! I have caught twelve leaves!'

Now the goblin began to pay attention. 'If you have caught twelve leaves, all different,' he said, 'that's magic.'

Tim spread his leaves on the grass and the goblin counted them.

'That one is a walnut leaf. And that's an oak leaf. This is a maple leaf. And that is from a silver birch. This one is from an apple tree. And that is a copper beech leaf. And here we have an ash leaf. And you also have a cob-nut leaf, a pear tree leaf, a rose leaf, a mulberry leaf and a fig leaf. You are a very lucky boy, Tim. You have caught twelve leaves, and all of them are different.'

from *A Leaf in the Shape of a Key* by Joan Aiken

Botanists at the Connecticut Aboretum declare that the elimination of beautiful native shrubs and wildflowers has reached the proportions of a 'roadside crisis'. Azaleas, mountain laurel, blueberries, huckleberries, viburnums, dogwood, bayberry, sweet fern, low shadbush, winterberry, chokeberry, and wild plum are dying before the chemical barrage. So are the daisies, black-eyed Susans, Queen Anne's lace, goldenrods, and autumn asters which lend grace and beauty to the landscape.

The spraying is not only improperly planned but studded with abuses such as these. In a southern New England town one contractor finished his work with some chemicals remaining in his tank. He discharged this along woodland roadsides where no spraying had been authorised. As a result the community lost the blue and golden beauty of its autumn roads, where asters and goldenrod would have made a display worth travelling far to see.

from *Silent Spring* by Rachel Carson

Lion

I saw a lion at the zoo.
His amber eyes stared distantly –
it seemed as if the paths and flowers,
the people, pushchairs, tidy trees,
were things he didn't see;
were things he didn't want to see.

And yet, cage-born, how could he know
how fast his hungry blood might flow,
the speed those pacing legs would learn –
to stalk, to chase, to wheel and turn,
across wide grasslands far away
if he were given liberty?

Pamela Gillilan

Stupidity Street

I saw with open eyes
Singing birds sweet
Sold in the shops
For the people to eat,
Sold in the shops of
Stupidity Street.

I saw in vision
The worm in the wheat,
And in the shops nothing
For people to eat;
Nothing for sale in
Stupidity Street.

Ralph Hodgson

A Sunlit Mirror

One time I was strolling by the river
When I saw a dragon flying. No, it was
A dragonfly, but the reflection made it massive.
Its river shadow shed its former outlook.

It shimmered gold in the sun, silver in the
moon and in the hazy mist of clouds it shines
brightly –
A lone lantern in a cruel world,
A soldier in a battlefield with the white
Light of sun and moon lifting him
Like a rainbowed
Warrior.

Adrian Ryder
The Vyne School

5

Greedy Green River

Now greedy green river has swallowed the sun,
Timid as twilight, the night creatures come.

Splodgy scuttlers, reeking of slime,
Darters, and burrowers with luminous eyes,
Scurrying twitterers, swoopers from trees,
With tails that tickle, or scales that gleam,
Or bristles that rustle like wind in dry leaves,

Timid as twilight, the night creatures come,
Now greedy green river has swallowed the sun.

Under the scum on duckweedy ponds
Frogspawn is foaming, tadpoles grow strong.
Toads creep stealthily out of the mud,
Crawl and wobble, and gobble the grubs.
Twigs flutter with moths. Bark oozes with slugs.

Timid as twilight, the night creatures come,
Now greedy green river has swallowed the sun.

Slow-worm wriggles his old bronze skin.
Water-rat plops like a furry fish,
Swimming, and nosing his way through the reeds.
Hedgehog sniffs ditches itchy with fleas
Then curls in a wasp-nest, and falls asleep

As the sun rises..
Rises..
Rises...

And birds dart out of the branches,
Swooping, wheeling, cackling and chattering,
Telling the world in a thousand languages:
Look at the light!

Look at the light!
Look at the light!

Leo Aylen

Philip unzipped the top pocket of his parka. He took out one of the dark seeds. He opened his fist so that it became a flat palm with the apple pip in the dip in his hand. He looked at the seed for a moment, his eyes fixed on it, seeing and yet not seeing. His palm seemed to stretch away from him as though focused through the wrong end of a telescope. A colour began to appear. The apple seed became royal blue with silver in it like razor-blades. The silver turned to shafts which beamed out on six sides with black-blue deepening between the shafts. It had a weight which Philip felt in his hand and could measure. He thought it equal to the weight of a March wind.

'I will plant it,' he said softly to himself. Then he heard himself say out loud, 'but this is the wrong time of the year. How can I plant a seed on Christmas Eve?'

The heaviness of the seed lowered his hand towards the earth.

'I will plant it,' he said to himself stubbornly, and in his head there seemed to be an echo from the oak and sycamore and hazel around him.

'I shouldn't .....' he argued aloud, but broke off as he felt the weight and texture and colour of the apple seed as it appeared to jump about and prickle in his hand.

'Of course I can plant it,' he heard himself say in a normal speaking voice.

Already while this odd dialogue was going on the heel of his wellington boot was scraping a hole in the soft damp soil.

continued

Philip dropped to his knees and scooped out the shallow hole rubbing the rich earth through his fingers. He carefully placed the seed in the bed. He watched enthralled as the royal blue almost black and the silver shafts mingled with the light reddish earth.

He gently sprinkled fine soil over the seed just as he'd seen his father do over seeds in the greenhouse.

Through the still and quiet morning a wind that was only just bigger than a breeze moved down the hill and over the field then into and among the trees. There it stopped.

Around Philip the oak and sycamore and even the smaller hazel seemed all at once, and in time, to dance a little shifting movement towards the spot where he had planted the apple seed. He knelt and dribbled a last handful of soil over the seed. As his hand emptied a silver dagger appeared to thrust out of the spot followed by a royal blue almost black handle.

from *Pictures in the Seed* by John Fairfax

Quetzals Only Come Once

The mother shakes the kaleidoscope,
holds it to the child's eye.
Swirls of blue deepen to purple
and black welling up. Silver flecks dart
through the shadows. She gives it a twist,
and a long path of light glitters
across it.

Ocean.
'Do another one.'

She shakes again. Shafts of fire
filter through screens of brown,
red, orange.

Autumn.
'What else
can you do?'

She shakes again,
and detonates green. Patterns of jade,
Lime, emerald, resolve
into a bird, a bright shiver
of greenness down its back,
its throat aflame.

Quetzal.
The child grabs: sends the pattern splintering.
'Make the quetzal again!'

She shakes her head.

'I can't:
quetzals only come once.'

Sheenagh Pugh

Fireweed in the Park

The park keeper hates us:
We sneak out when he's not looking
And tell scarlet stories so shocking
That all the dusty old women
Start sneezing at once;
They trap the keeper in his hut,
Bang on his door with sticks,
Shout through his letter box
And threaten to do him a mischief;
So he rushes out in a rage
And chops and slashes and burns
And thinks he's done the trick.

What a laugh!
We've grown feathers,
Turned into a flock of doves,
And flown high over the fence.

Now we look for earth,
Earth as dark as a magician's hat.

David Orme

9

Greater Spotted Woodpecker

this is smaller than the green one tho its habits are
the same   it is of a pied color of brown and white
with a red crown and a dingy hue of red on the
under parts of the belly – it taps more frequently on
the trees then the green one but is not so often seen
as it generally keeps about the tops of the trees and
makes the hole for its nest in the grains   I know
nothing of its eggs as I never have had as yet the
good fortune to meet with a nest – it seems to have
a quick ear at the approach of any thing from which
it seldom flyes but nimbles on the other side of the
grain out of sight – there is a smaller one of the same
color as this (lesser spotted woodpecker) but not so
common   I have seen it often but know nothing of
its habits any way different from the former

When Woodpeckers are making or boring their
holes in the spring they are so attentive over their
labours that they are easily caught by boys who
watch them when they are half hid in the holes they
are making and climbing softly up the tree make
them prisoners – as nest thus left unfinished is never
resumed by another – the male makes the holes
generally and when finished sets up a continued cry
to invite a companion that seldom fails to join him
in seeking materials for lining the nest – the pied
woodpecker never bores holes in the body of the
tree but in the larger grains very high up and always
on the underneath side so that they are inaccesable
to nest hunting boys – it is easy to see where this
tribe are making new nests by the litter they make at
the foot of the tree as if it where sawdust

John Clare

Greater Spotted

Woodpecker comes to break bread
swanning in for high table, the
mark of the goddess upon him

waxing lyrical on the rust
gingham of his wiry nut-sac and
crossing out its tawny noughts.

Tailfeathers fan their black and white
crazy-paving spotted with blood. His
top hat slips, breast swells like a

full sail or new-lain egg as he
taps anew at a crust's closed door.
Broody wagtail lands and leaves

out of his depth. Greenfinch and
yellow-hammer throw out complaints
on a wing and a prayer.

Only the humble sparrow remains,
falling like a pebble on discarded
scraps: flung nuts, flown crumbs.

Humbler still, I hold vigil from an
open window in secret courtship,
knowing the drill.

Sue Stewart

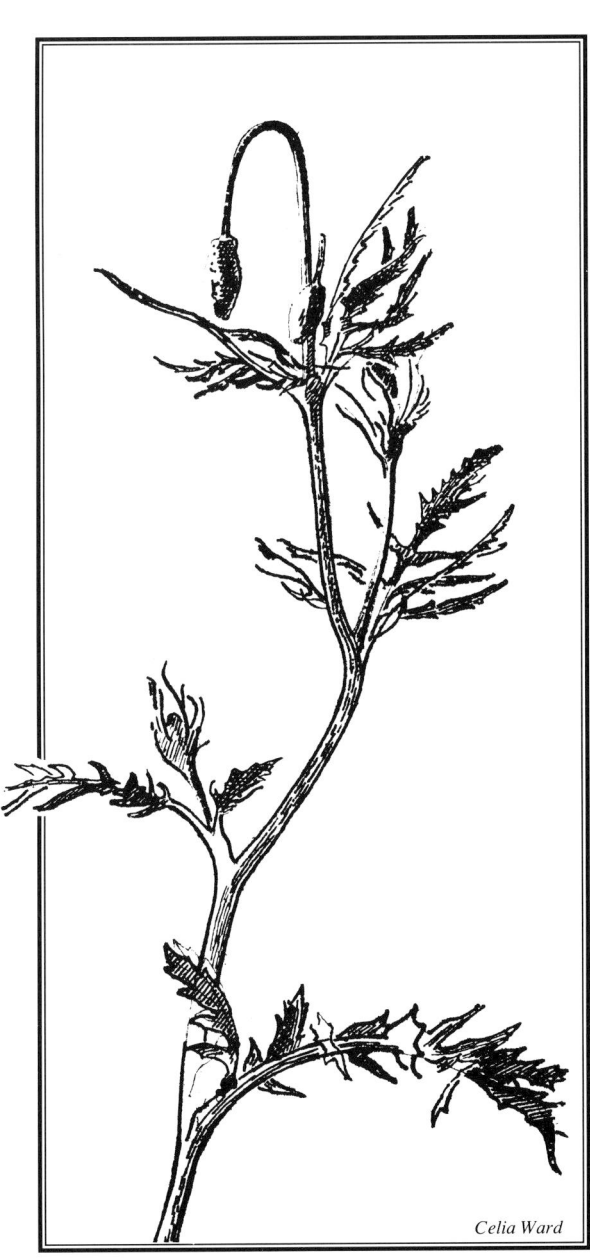

Celia Ward

Interview with painter Celia Ward

SS: Celia, I know you do a lot of landscape work. Do you like painting out of doors in this way?

CW: Yes, I do. I've never felt better than after a long spell working out of doors. You just feel so healthy when you come in at the end of the day. To paint landscape I, and I think many other painters, sit quietly and still for long periods of time in the same spot, so animals and insects and birds get used to your presence and cease to be afraid. Rabbits come quite close to you and, if I'm painting a river, dragonflies will often actually rest on my paper. Butterflies too move very close. There's a wonderful sense of being within a living countryside. Also if you are outside you get very very cold sometimes, and wet, but this can be exhilarating too.

SS: Would you always rather draw plants in their natural habitat?

CW: Yes, because for me the natural background of plants are usually the most beautiful. A primrose looks loveliest in a bank, a bluebell inside a wood, a dog rose in a hedgerow. They are at their most luscious when seen outside.

SS: If you found some bluebells to paint, would you go hunting for the best ones?

CW: I would paint any bluebell that I thought looked interesting. I don't worry if a plant has been partially eaten by insects. Many have, and it often adds variety of shape to the drawing. In many old drawings, in fact, insects are drawn *on* the plants. Some botanical draftsmen paint only plants that are in perfect condition. This is fairly unnatural, and I enjoy the irregularities of bitten holes.

SS: Do you ever draw gardens, or do you prefer woods and wild flowers?

CW: Yes, I prefer the wild. I find cultivated plants often have very strong colours, too strong. You get fierce reds and fierce pinks, which I find garish to paint in comparison with the pale pinks of the dog rose.

SS: Would you ever bring plants and flowers indoors to paint?

CW: I've never been much interested in painting vases of flowers. The magic of the rose for me is the rose that grows on the bush. It's the mixture of those strong branches, the thorns, and the terribly delicate flowers, that is magical, I find. Foxgloves, too, are wonderful to paint in the wild.

SS: But if you wanted to paint a flower in great detail, perhaps one that grows close to the ground, would you pick it then?

CW: Yes, I would if I was painting a botanical drawing of the flower, that is, a drawing done in a very realistic way so that we will know exactly what kind of flower it is. A primrose I will paint so that we *know* it is a primrose, it will have the right number of petals and stamens, and will be the true colour. What I do is I pick the plant and lay it on the drawing paper and then draw a picture of it next to the actual plant. You have to get to know how long each flower will last out of water, and as soon as you've finished drawing it you put it back into the water so it can drink some more and stay alive.

SS: Would you say that this kind of drawing was more scientific than artistic?

CW: It is both. Leonardo, who must have drawn some of the greatest botanical drawings, was both scientist and artist. The arrangement can be beautifully done so that the leaves are placed interestingly on the page and the details picked out in a manner to make a good design. Scientists today still use drawings to identify plants.

SS: How did botanical drawing begin?

CW: The Greeks produced botanical drawings in the fourth century B.C., and there was much botanical drawing during the Middle Ages. Plants needed to be recorded accurately for medical reasons. Doctors or herbalists had drawn records of the plants they needed to cure people with.

SS: How long does it take you to draw a flower?

CW: To draw one flower, say a primrose, I suppose would take an hour or two to do it scientifically. But to draw a whole bush, say with ten branches, many leaves and lots of roses, might take a complete week. There's such a variety of leaf, each one a different colour and shape, the light falling on each in a different manner. Each flower, too, is a different size and colour, some closed up in bud, some virtually dead, some opening. It is this variety that creates a sense of enormous liveliness within a picture if you can capture it.

Jan

Meet Jan, he lives on the top of a hill
with a pet goat he won't name
and a white hen he treats the same.
If you won't meet him, others will –

like Norman Bates over there, talking
to the girl with orange hair,
he's already been up there
at Jan's. Ask him, he'll tell you walking

is the only way to get there,
the road stops a mile away,
and then you hack your way
through rhododendrons, and there

in front of you, is Jan's windmill
painted black, with sails turning
to keep Jan's lights burning
and his hi-fi playing. Come on, he'll

greet you with goat's milk, and eggs
and maybe fresh fruit
from his plot, but no meat.
Keep your eye off his hen's legs.

Look, instead, at how fit Jan is
up there on his hill farm
doing the world no harm –
the world that could live as Jan does.

Matthew Sweeney

Fay Godwin / Network

There were on the planet where the little prince lived – as on all planets – good plants and bad plants. In consequence, there were good seeds from good plants, and bad seeds from bad plants. But seeds are invisible. They sleep deep in the heart of the earth's darkness, until some one among them is seized with the desire to awaken. Then this little seed will stretch itself and begin – timidly at first – to push a charming little sprig inoffensively upward toward the sun. If it is only a sprout of radish or the sprig of a rose-bush, one would let it grow wherever it might wish. But when it is a bad plant, one must destroy it as soon as possible, the very first instant that one recognises it.

Now there were some terrible seeds on the planet that was the home of the little prince; and these were the seeds of the baobab. The soil of that planet was infested with them. A baobab is something you will never, never be able to get rid of if you attend to it too late. It spreads over the entire planet. It bores clear through it with its roots. And if the planet is too small and the baobabs are too many, they split it in pieces . . .

'It is a question of discipline,' the little prince said to me later on. 'When you've finished your own toilet in the morning, then it is time to attend to the toilet of your planet, just so, with the greatest care. You must see to it that you pull up regularly all the baobabs, at the very first moment when they can be distinguished from the rose-bushes which they resemble so closely in their earliest youth. It is very tedious work,' the little prince added. 'but very easy.'

And one day he said to me: 'You ought to make a beautiful drawing, so that the children where you live can see exactly how all this is. That would be very useful to them if they were to travel some day.

'Sometimes,' he added, 'there is no harm in putting off a piece of work until another day. But when it is a matter of baobabs, that always means a catastrophe. I knew a planet that was inhabited by a lazy man. He neglected three little bushes . . .'

So, as the little prince described it to me, I have made a drawing of that planet. I do not much like to take the tone of a moralist. But the danger of the baobabs is so little understood, and such considerable risks would be run by anyone who might get lost on an asteroid, that for once I am breaking though my reserve. 'Children,' I say plainly, 'watch out for the baobabs!'

My friends, like myself, have been skirting this danger for a long time, without ever knowing it; and so it is for them that I have worked so hard over this drawing. The lesson which I pass on by this means is worth all the trouble it has cost me.

Perhaps you will ask me, 'Why there are no other drawings in this book as magnificent and impressive as this drawing of the baobabs?'

The reply is simple. I have tried. But with the others I have not been successful. When I made the drawing of the baobabs I was carried beyond myself by the inspiring force of urgent necessity.

Activities

Class discussion

The writing in this section shows how closely writers, artists and scientists have to observe the world around them. Read again the interview with the painter Celia Ward. How does she help you to 'see' the world more clearly?

Discuss ways in which artists and scientists are (a) similar and (b) different in their approach to the natural world.

Which poems in *The world's a paintbox* show that the poets are good observers?

Group activities

Read 'The Buttercup Experiment' poem by Wes Magee. Do you use flowers or plants for other 'experiments' – daisies, blades of grass, dock leaves, sycamore seeds? Swap ideas, then write a poem about the best one.

Choose one piece of writing or poem which seems to be a 'warning' to human beings. Discuss what the 'warning' might be, then present your ideas to the class, beginning by reading aloud the piece of writing. Practise your performance carefully.

Pair activities

Not all poems are easy to understand the first time you read them! In pairs, choose a poem that you find quite difficult and write a list of questions you would like to ask the writer.

Read out your questions to the class: they may be able to help you find the answers.

Read the extract from *A Leaf in the Shape of a Key* by Joan Aiken and compare it with President Reagan's comment, quoted in Jonathan Porritt's Schumacher Lecture. Which do you agree with?

Write a poem about flowers, showing these two different viewpoints. You might like to alternate the lines, so that you each take one side. Or you could have a repeating line (a 'refrain') to show the Reagan viewpoint. Make it a funny poem if you like.

Individual writing

John Fairfax, who wrote *Pictures in the Seed*, says that 'Each seed holds in it the magic of what it might become.' Look closely at some seeds: if no real seeds are available, look at the drawings of seeds below. Write about what they might grow into. Be as imaginative as you like: remember the story of Jack and the Beanstalk!

Read again John Clare's description of the woodpecker, then the poem 'Greater Spotted' on page 10. (The description by John Clare uses *his* spelling and punctuation, although you will find several mistakes here. Spaces are used instead of full stops.)

'A Sunlit Mirror' and 'Lion' do not have a prose description to pair with them. Choose one these poems and write a 'scientific' description of the creature it describes. Use a reference book for your information.

 The pieces in this section are full of interesting and unusual words. Choose five to ten interesting words from one poem or extract and use them in a piece of writing of your own.

 Look carefully at the two stanzas in 'Stupidity Street'.

Look at:
> the rhyme pattern
> the pattern of the first line
> the pattern of the last two lines.

Now write an extra stanza of your own.

 Read the poem 'Fireweed in the Park' by David Orme. What are the 'feathers' he mentions? Write about another weed that spreads masses of fluffy seeds: a dandelion, for instance, or a thistle.

Extension

Dennis Craig's poem 'Flowers' shows how an unpleasant, slum area of a city was completely transformed when a park was created.

Elsewhere, even in the countryside, you will find scruffy, unattractive places. Find such a place near you and draw up a plan for improving it, for the benefit of the people who live there and for wildlife. You will need to include plans and maps as well as a description of how the project might be tackled. You could include poems describing the place 'before' and 'after'.

Turn on the tap

The Puddle

I look in the puddle, what do I see?
My reflection all weird and shimmering.
The grass sways in the light end-of-July breeze.
When the water turns muddy with gravel,
You cannot see the lovely reflections.
When the muddy puddle
clears, a wobble returns.

Sally Anne Marsh
The Vyne School

Composer

On the first floor the boy with the drum kit
Pounds and crashes like an angry ocean.
Upstairs in David's tidy garret
Spools unwind a slower music
He has woven from birdsong,
Bowed strings, high-pitched stones.

Walking at low tide beside the river,
Attentive to driftwood, summer grasses,
To the flowering of unchecked branches
And to wind-blown patterns on the water,
He gathers details from the afternoon
And makes of these another remedy.

Wendy Cope

What Rain Does

We don't need to water flowers,
   The rain is a watering can,
   The rain is a hose.
We don't need to sweep the path,
   The rain is a broom.
You may get a shock
If the rain splashes you
Making your skirts and trousers wet
Like a washing machine,
Washing all the dirt out.
That is what the rain does.
Don't wash your windows,
The rain is your window cloth.

Fiona Pearson
Oakridge Junior School

Dipper

No webbed feet,
but a water bird for all that.

And a gentlemanly one –
he walks on the bottom
of his helter-skelter stream
wearing a white shirt-front
and a brown cummerbund.

He hates dry land.
He flies up a twisty stream
following the twists
all the way.

When he perches on a stone
it's a wet one.
He stands there, bobbing and bobbing
as though the water's applauding him.

He likes his nest
to be behind a rippling tapestry –
a tapestry? Well,
a waterfall.

Naturally.

Norman MacCaig

Ice

Isn't it nice
To know that ice
Floats at the top of the water?

At about four degrees,
When it's starting to freeze,
The cold liquid begins to rise
To the top of the pond
Where it soon forms a bond
Of ice, like a lid on the water.
So although it gets dim
The watery creatures can swim
Safe under it,
From frost and from snow.
Until Spring brings the sun
And life's rebegun
When the rivers and streams are aflow.

If it weren't for that
Neat arrangement, my dear,
None of us,
Not one of us,
Would be here!

John Cotton

It's Poisoning Down

Granny keeps telling stories
Of how she used to go
Walking in the pouring rain
And playing in the snow.
She talks of things called flowers,
She says they had nice smells.
(Sometimes she sounds convincing,
The crazy fibs she tells!)
She says that lakes and rivers
Were once all clean and pure,
But I don't believe a word,
I've heard it all before.
Poor Gran can be quite dotty –
You want to see Mum frown
When she tries to get outside
Even though it's poisoning down.

We've had to fit 'Granny Locks'
To keep poor Granny in.
She really doesn't understand
How rain eats away the skin.

Brian Patten

Third-world War

The beach, walking off
inland, dragging its bed of
sand. And look, no guns!

Food-chain

The feeding over:
one eye hard and accusing –
fish out of water.

E A Markham

Rain Magic

Gentle breeze is the father of rain,
Soft wind is the father of cloudburst.
Rain will not drench me today;
Rain will pack its belongings and go away.
 The antelope is humming,
 The buffalo is grumbling,
 The pig grunts in its belly.
Words have angered the red monkey,
But today he was given the right words
And his anger will disappear.

Yoruba, Nigeria

There's thunder in the air.
Danger surrounds the child
Peering through the window
At the teeming rain.
Lightning plays across the sky,
Sliding hither and thither,
Pyrotechnical zigzags, becoming
A maze in the sky. Thunder
Gives a sudden hacking cough,
And another and yet another.
The sky is infested;
Electric snakes swarm the earth.
A man runs across fields,
Metal glinting brightly on his coat.
An electric dart currents home,
Crackling into his heart.
The child's features, startled in the
Window, vanish into the house.

Kim Stock

Wet

The road is a river, the trees beat rain,
everything's on fire.
My golden roses smoked to dawn,
the muck-heap steamed in the stable-yard.
These hills were boiling. Whirling, old,
the earth is not yet cold.

Alison Brackenbury

Westwood St Thomas' School

The fog was thinning now under the heat of the sun that shone bare above on the peak in a bright sky. As the mists moved and parted in great drifts and smoky wisps, the villagers saw a band of warriors coming up the mountain. They were armoured with bronze helmets and greaves and breastplates of heavy leather and shields of wood and bronze, and armed with swords and the long Kargish lance. Winding up along the steep bank of the Ar they came in a plumed, clanking, straggling line, near enough already that their white faces could be seen, and the words of their jargon heard as they shouted to one another. In this band of the invading horde there were about a hundred men, which is not many; but in the village were only eighteen men and boys.

Now need called knowledge out: Duny, seeing the fog blow and thin across the path before the Kargs, saw a spell that might avail him. An old weatherworker of the Vale, seeking to win the boy as prentice, had taught him several charms. One of these tricks was called fogweaving, a binding-spell that gathers the mists together for a while in one place; with it one skilled in illusion can shape the mist into fair ghostly seemings, which last a little and fade away. The boy had no such skill, but his intent was different, and he had the strength to turn the spell to his own ends. Rapidly and aloud he named the places and the boundaries of the village, and then spoke the fogweaving charm, but in among its words he enlaced the words of a spell of concealment, and last he cried the word that set the magic going.

Even as he did so his father coming up behind him struck him hard on the side of the head, knocking him right down. 'Be still, fool! Keep your blattering mouth shut, and hide if you can't fight!'

continued

Duny got to his feet. He could hear the Kargs now at the end of the village, as near as the great yew-tree by the tanner's yard. Their voices were clear, and the clink and creak of their harness and arms, but they could not be seen. The fog had closed and thickened all over the village, greying the light, blurring the world till a man could hardly see his own hands before him.

'I've hidden us all,' Duny said, sullenly, for his head hurt from his father's blow, and the working of the doubled incantation had drained his strength. 'I'll keep up this fog as long as I can. Get the others to lead them up to High Fall.'

The smith stared at his son who stood wraithlike in that weird, dank mist. It took him a minute to see Duny's meaning, but when he did he ran at once, noiselessly, knowing every fence and corner of the village, to find the others and tell them what to do.

from *A Wizard of Earthsea* by Ursula le Guin

CROFT DHU, INVERNESS-SHIRE

Water, for instance, the sheer innocent beauty of it. Lately in my glass – and who says that it is odourless and tasteless? Its taste is inspiring, untainted here by chemical of any kind, clear, full-shouldered, aching with peat and mica, schist-clean, grass-rooted, out-of-clouds, hailwater, sheepwater, bluewater. Preserving in itself the storm, the blizzards, the February snow.

And the water in this house, a miracle of engineering. When I turned it on at the stopcock the other day, it crept past the valves and sniffed out a strange dryness in the pipe ... then fingers and toes it edged round the first corner, before gathering courage and hurling itself into the house-pipes and finally – miracle out of the taps – this clear green or was it blue standing down into the big white bath and basin.

And the bath, I fill it to the brim with hot water, until I am a submerged reef and the water-light breaks over my pinkish stone. It stands like a green field in this enamel; winking, surging, breaking into new patterns. I flex it underneath my spine ... there, a warm pair of hands massaging the crooks in my back.

Harry Laing

Boxer's Lake

Boxer's Lake is dying.
(Does Mr Boxer know?)
The place I caught my carpfish
two score years ago.

My world of grass and rushes,
my world of bread and paste,
setting sun in ripples,
running home – too late.
Yes,
Boxer's Lake is dying
tombstone floating fish,
white as water lily
white as morning mist . . .

white as bankside parsley
white stone bulging eyes
jogging in the rushes
jogging with the flies.

Yes,

Boxer's Lake is dying
another world is dead

. . .

it did not make a profit
and a price was on its head.

Peter Dixon

The Sea Moaning

I'm sick of being slicked,
had enough of sticky stuff.
I don't need oiling any more than
you need filling up with fluff.

I'm through with sewage,
had it up to here with poo.
I don't need fertilising any more than
you need 'flu.

I'm done with tons of tins,
not got with a lotta bobbing lobbed bottles.
I don't need trashing any more than
you need your tongue knotted.

I'm well malaised by radiation,
truly waned by uranium.
I don't need nuking any more than
you need geraniums in your cranium.

So, humans, I'm in a huff;
my lovely blue is in a stew.
If all that moves within me's throttled
it's only thanks to you,

Brains!

Adam Thorpe

Chart Topper

Weatherman, weatherman,
we've had enough of your
rain patches, cloud batches;

your snap blizzards, way out hazards,
bump storms
and scarey foghorns –

(AND we don't want another dinosaur
like Hurricane Hetty
or Coldfront Yeti).

Weatherman, weatherman,
cut out the blather, man –
from this time on

we don't need perks
like cold toes, red noses,
clammy collars, soggy socks.

Weatherman, weatherman,
get it together, man –
do one simple thing for us

send us some blue.

Geoffrey Holloway

THE RISING SEA OF CHANGE

As the world warms up because of the greenhouse effect, scientists are worried that sea levels will rise as a result. It was generally thought that sea levels might rise by about a metre by the year 2010. Now some American scientists say they think they got their sums wrong.

Trying to work out how much sea levels will rise is very complicated. It also takes a great deal of guess work.

All sorts of things affect the sea level, so it's not surprising that scientists aren't certain exactly what will happen.

To begin with nobody can really be sure how much the atmosphere will warm up. The amount of warming depends on how much carbon dioxide – that's the gas that is the main cause of the greenhouse effect – will be released.

Once you've made your best guess about that you can work out roughly how much the atmosphere will warm up. Then you have to estimate how much the sea will warm up.

When water warms up it expands – it takes up more space. The sea is so deep that even a tiny amount of warming will mean the water level rises enough to worry about.

And if both the atmosphere and the sea water warm up, they will affect the ice at the Earth's poles. The more warming there is, the faster the ice will melt. This too will affect the sea level.

Trying to calculate all these effects is difficult enough. But even more difficult is guessing what will happen to our weather. You might think that if the air is warmer, then there will be less snow falling on the North and South poles. But that isn't the case.

In fact rain and snow are often caused by warm wet air being cooled down. The cool air can't absorb the water vapour so the extra water vapour forms clouds and then falls as rain.

According to the American scientists, the biggest change to their estimates is because they have changed their calculations about how much carbon dioxide will be released. The latest estimate is that this won't be as much as was previously thought.

As a result they now say that the sea level may only rise by half as much as they previously thought. That could be good news for all those countries that risk being badly flooded.

But the scientists admit their calculations are based on a great many guesses. Nobody can be really sure what is going to happen.

The Formation of the The Clarence River, New South Wales

In New South Wales, the Clarence River rises in the mountains near the Queensland border and enters the sea at Yamba. The story which follows form part of the Aboriginal history of the making of the Clarence River by the wicked old woman of the Creation period, Dirrangun.

Some people say that Dirrangun is a witch, that she's mean and cunning and brings you all the mischief in the world. Others say that she's friendly. But she's a very old woman and she has long hair down to her knees.

Dirrangun had two married daughters and a son-in-law. This son-in-law was a Buloogan, a strong handsome man. The daughters of the Dirrangun were his two wives. The daughters quarrelled with their mother and the Buloogan took the quarrel up and sided with his wives. They starved the old woman; they didn't pass her anything to eat and she became angry.

continued

Dirrangun's camp was under a big fig tree at the waterfall which is the source of the Clarence River. There was a basin, a hollow in the rock, which contained their water. Dooloomi was the name of the pool, and it was the jurraveel or home of the spirit of the water. Tooloom now is the white man's name for this waterfall – Tooloom is the nearest he could get to saying Dooloomi.

While the son-in-law and his two wives were out hunting and gathering food, Dirrangun drained all the water out of the pool with a bark coolamon, or carrying dish. When the Buloogan and his two wives came home in the evening, there was no water. The two wives were running about all over the place looking for water, but there was no water. Dirrangun had put leaves and bark over the empty basin hole in the rock so that the place was hidden. For two or three days the Buloogan and his wives could not get a drink of water and they became desperately thirsty.

Dirrangun was pretending to cry for them. Some people say that Dirrangun was sitting on this coolamon of water in her camp, hiding it, and that when the Buloogan found this out, he got angry and cried, 'Well, you're not going to have all the water! I'll let it out!' He thrust his spear into that coolamon and let it out.

Others say that when Dirrangun, the Buloogan and his two wives went to sleep, the Buloogan's two dogs, who were thirsty, found the water which Dirrangun had hidden in the coolamon. Two mountains nearby, called Dillalea and Kalloo-Guthun, are named after those two dogs. In the night the dogs returned to the camp of the Buloogan and stood over him. And the water dripped from their mouths. When the Buloogan felt this he woke up and followed the two dogs back to where Dirrangun was asleep with the hidden water.

When the Buloogan saw where the water was hidden, he was angry. He caused heavy rain to fall and the hollow rock-basin began to fill. The water rose and rose and backed up where the creek is now.

When the water began to rise Dirrangun climbed into the fig tree and made a platform in the boughs. But the water rose and swept her and the fig tree away and left a hollow beneath the cliffs where the waterfall is now. Dirrangun was holding on to the fig tree as she was swept away. She was swept over the second fall, which we call Ngalumbeh. At the bottom of this fall she was whirled around and round, still holding on to the fig tree, in a whirlpool for half a day.

The water was getting stronger and stronger. The Buloogan had cursed the water to make it unmanageable. It took her and the fig tree away down into the Clarence River. From time to time Dirrangun would sit in the torrent with her legs wide apart trying to block the water, but each time the flood would bear her away. Where the South River comes into the Clarence River, Dirrangun sat with her legs outspread. The water rose and went up and made the South River. There she sat until the flood rose and swept her and the fig tree on again.

Below Grafton, on the river, there is a fig tree growing. Many old men would see that fig tree and say, 'Oh, look! Dooloomi borrgun!' which means, 'That fig tree belongs to Tooloom!' Those old men would say, 'Dirrangun. She's away down there, but she belongs up there at Tooloom.' But Dirrangun is still in that fig tree below Grafton.

Eustan Williams, Githavul tribe

Activities

Class discussion

Look again at Jonathan Fairfax's comic strip. Why does the bird change her mind about the mucky seawater?

Have you ever had to 'choose between two evils' in this way? (It doesn't have to be a life-or-death situation!) Can you talk about it to the rest of the class?

Read 'The Formation of the Clarence River, New South Wales'. As they grow up, the Aborigines listen to these stories so often that they remember them easily, and pass them on to the younger ones. This is their 'oral tradition' (passed on by spoken word), and it goes back 40,000 years.

Are there any stories you've heard that you can remember word for word? It might be a fairy tale, a nursery rhyme, or a story your mother or father made up for you. Perhaps many of you remember the same story: if so, see if you tell it the same way.

Group activities

Take a close look at Linda Combi's drawing of Dirrangun and the Clarence River, from the Aboriginal story. Everything in it represents a part of nature. In groups, see if you can work out what the different symbols stand for.

When you think you know what they mean, see if you can make your own symbolic myth drawings. Work in a group or on your own, whichever you prefer. Use a favourite story or myth, and make up your symbols as you go along.

Rain isn't always popular! Write a group poem, alternating the lines with things that are good about rain, and things that are not so good . . .

> It waters the thirsty soil,
> It drums hard on my face . . .
> etc.

The Yoruba poem 'Rain Magic' is a spell to make the rain vanish. In small groups, write your own spell to bring the rain back.

Pair activities

Design either a funny picture ('cartoon'), or a comic strip, to illustrate an issue you feel strongly about. Have the spoken words either underneath your picture/s, or in speech bubbles.

Wendy Cope's poem 'Composer' shows that there are many sounds in nature made by birds, sea and wind. Thunder, lightning and rain are noisy too, and so are animals. Write a 'noisy story' together, bringing in as many of these sounds as you can. Go over the story several times to make sure you're happy with it.

Then, if you're able to, record your story on a tape recorder, including sound effects. Use musical instruments to help you.

Individual writing

 Read the journal extract, 'Croft Dhu, Inverness-shire'. Harry Laing says of this piece:

'If water was alive (which of course it is!) what kind of animal would it be? Would it look like all the places it came from? I was thinking about this as I turned on the tap and when I got into the bath – I knew the answer.'

Water comes in many shapes and sizes, from a pond to a waterfall. See how many you can list, and think about what kind of animals they might be. (A raindrop could be a mouse, a river a cheetah . . .) Then write a poem about one of them, using the animal idea throughout the poem.

Read again John Cotton's poem 'Ice'. What scientific information does the poem give us about water turning into ice?

Using reference books, find out how one thing can change into another: for instance seeds turn into flowers, eggs turn into chickens. When you've found an idea you like, write a poem, including as much information as you can.

Adam Thorpe says of his poem 'The Sea Moaning':

'I wanted to get over how it must feel to be the sea, a living being full of this nasty stuff we oafs chuck in: a kind of slow torture.'

If this is how the sea feels, how do you think other things in nature might feel? Write a poem as if you were one of them: you might choose to be another element, such as air, or you might want to be an oak tree, or a snake, or a bamboo stalk. It could be a happy poem, or an unhappy poem.

Read 'What Rain Does' by Fiona Pearson. This poem is full of metaphors: how many can you find?

Now write a poem on 'What the Wind Does', using as many metaphors as you can. For instance, 'The wind is a monkey, rustling the leaves, The wind is a temper, raising the roof . . . '

Brian Patten's poem 'It's Poisoning Down' is written in an 'ironic' tone. Discuss what irony means with your teacher, then write a poem about an issue that troubles you, using the ironic tone to get your message across.

Extension

Imagine there's a drought and we all need to save water. You've been put in charge of publicity. Think of the ways we use water: garden hoses, car washes, baths and showers, washing machines, washing up, filling kettles, etc. Then devise a Save Water Campaign, designing posters, information packs, news bulletins and displays.

Songs of the wild

Song of the Animal World

SOLOIST	The fish goes . . .	(Chorus) Hip!
	The bird goes . . .	Viss!
	The monkey goes . . .	Gnan!
FISH	I start to the left,	
	I twist to the right,	
	I am the fish	
	That slips through the water,	
	That slides,	
	That twists,	
	That leaps!	
SOLOIST	Everything lives,	
	Everything dances,	
	Everything sings:	
	The fish goes . . .	(Chorus) Hip!
	The bird goes . . .	Viss!
	The monkey goes . . .	Gnan!
BIRD	The bird flies away,	
	Flies, flies, flies,	
	Goes, returns, passes,	
	Climbs, floats, swoops.	
	I am the bird!	
SOLOIST	Everything lives,	
	Everything dances,	
	Everything sings:	
	The fish goes . . .	(Chorus) Hip!
	The bird goes . . .	Viss!
	The monkey goes . . .	Gnan!
MONKEY	The monkey! From branch to branch	
	Runs, hops, jumps,	
	With his wife and baby,	
	Mouth stuffed full, tail in air,	
	Here's the monkey! Here's the monkey!	
SOLOIST	Everything lives,	
	Everything dances,	
	Everything sings:	
	The fish goes . . .	(Chorus) Hip!
	The bird goes . . .	Viss!
	The monkey goes . . .	Gnan!

Zaire, Central Africa

Riverside Cabaret

Close to the city
a stile and a footpath
lead from the clatter
of traffic and street.
Out of a culvert
a cool stream is running
down into woodland
tumbling free.

The air in the valley
is pungent with blossom
of meadowsweet, myrtle,
bramble and briar.
Hornet and hoverfly
hum a deep chorus,
cricket and grasshopper
drum for the choir.

Chaffinch is practising
concert cadenzas.
Blackbird joins in
with arpeggios, trills.
Pond-skaters polka
on whirlpools of water;
fishes are spinning
head over heels.

Curtains of willow
sway to the rhythm;
glimpses of colour
appear through the leaves.
With rustle of wings
like paper fans clapping
a flurry of jewels
is spilled on the breeze.

Ruby and topaz,
amethyst, sapphire,
glowing, pulsating,
emerald, pearl;
capering sunbeams
twist on a rainbow:
over the river
dragonflies whirl.

Edna Eglinton

The Poet and the Trees

The poet sat at his desk;
he just couldn't get it right.
It was five o'clock in the morning
and he'd been there all night.

There was paper on the desk,
there was paper on the floor,
there was paper in the wastebins,
there was more and more and more.

By now he couldn't see his desk
and the mountain of paper was rocking,
when suddenly outside his door
a crowd of trees came knocking.

'We're very, very angry!'
said the tallest of the trees.
The others nodded in agreement
like cornfields in a breeze.

I found the poet at his desk.
He was very, very dead
and the trees had carved this poem
on the desk beside his head:

'Words are precious.
Poems are paper,
paper is trees,
so think about it,
please.'

Martyn Wiley and Ian McMillan

STORM'S THREE MILLION VICTIMS

At least three million trees were blown down during Britain's latest storms.

According to the Forestry Commission, responsible for large areas of the country's woodlands, the winds wrecked forests across southern England and Wales. Somerset, Cornwall, Avon and Wiltshire were the worst hit, and one in every 20 trees on Dartmoor were lost or damaged.

There were also substantial losses in Dorset and Shropshire, and in Wales and the eastern counties.

Mr David Foot, operations director, said: 'It already seems clear that the forest damage is very substantial, although not on quite the same scale as the losses we incurred in 1987.'

Early Times, 8 February 1990

New Town

Birds don't sing where we live any more.
The Council rooted up the trees there used to be before,
Elder and sycamore and hazel and birch.
There's nowhere in our district for the birds to perch.

The Council laid down concrete roads and made up woody names,
Grove Lane and Copse Hill and that kind of thing.
All right for traffic and cross-last games
But there's nowhere for birds to build their nests and sing.

Sparrows didn't mind and pigeons didn't mind.
They're the only sort left; they stayed behind.
But blackbirds and chaffinches and wrens are gone for good.
You don't hear them sing now in our neighbourhood.

Joan Aiken

Meadow Avenue

The yields
of fields
were cows and crops

But now
No cows:
Just streets & shops.

Trevor Millum

Interview with sculptor Michael Fairfax

SS: Michael, as a sculptor you use wood, stone and metal, but you work mainly in wood, don't you?

MF: Yes, I have a very strong affinity with wood, having been brought up in the countryside where I spent most of my time in the woods walking and playing. When I work in woods now I just get sheer delight from seeing the trees and plants, the different seasons. It doesn't matter if it's cold or hot, if the wind's blowing or whatever, you just enjoy each day, just being there and working with the wood that grows there.

SS: How do you decide which tree to use?

MF: When you see a tree growing in a particular shape, you might decide to use that shape for a sculpture. You can pick and choose what shape you want. Also you'll use a tree for its particular quality. You'll use a chestnut for its cleaving qualities, and also for the fact that it lasts outside as a wood for many years without having any treatment, and the same with oak, whereas if you use sycamore it will die and go back into the earth much more quickly. Willow will propagate very quickly, so you can put staves of willow in the ground and use it as part of a growing sculpture. Every place you go has its own type of soil, its own type of tree, and this dictates the kind of sculpture you'll make. So you don't go in there with fixed ideas, you let nature tell you what to make. That's a thing I really like about working in different areas – Somerset, Sussex, Kent, Wales – you look at the conditions of the land.

SS: Do you ever feel sad that you have to cut a tree down in order to make a sculpture?

MF: If I do cut down a tree then there are several things I can do to make up for that. One is that I can coppice the tree, so it can carry on growing from the bottom. That's a very traditional element of tree husbandry in Britain. I'll sometimes use a tree which is being strangled by vine and so it's slowly dying at the top, and again I coppice it so it can grow back. Also, I cut down a large oak tree in Somerset, and felling it brought so much light into the woodland that all the little saplings there had more chance to grow. Also, within quite a few sculptures that I've made I'll incorporate planting schemes, where I'm actually planting new trees into the sculpture. So in fact for someone who's known as a wood sculptor, I've probably put more wood back into the landscape than I've taken from it.

SS: You've also done some work for the conservation project run by Common Ground called 'Trees, Woods and the Green Man'. Can you tell us about this?

Farewell drawing for kiln wood.
Including various sculptures and features of my time there.

Various foliage.
Acorns - Grasses
- leaves.

Ship with wings

Trees rattle too.

the wren
that nested.
in the roots
near - Ship
with wings.

the water trickles
gently down her
back.

Throne for
a Blackboy

Lovers Shrine.

Moonshrine

MF: Yes, this was in Kiln Wood at Blackboys in East Sussex, and I was to work in the wood there for six months, getting to know the environment and making my sculptures. During this time of course – this was in 1987 – we had the Great Wind of October 17th which blew down eighty per cent of the trees in the wood I was working in. None of the sculptures got damaged though one had a huge oak limb lying across the top of it, which I managed to move. But because of the storm Common Ground decided to extend the project for three months until the following spring when the trees would be coming back to life again. During that time I made a series of sculptures to do with regeneration. If a fallen tree had part of its roots still in the ground, I would coppice or ringbark it so it could send up new shoots and grow into a new tree. The old tree, the fallen one, I would then make into a sculpture. So in years to come you'd have a horizontal sculpture and a new, vertical tree, with the roots half in and half out of the ground.

SS: Your sculptures always blend in with the landscape, rather than competing with it, and this is something Common Ground encourages artists to do. Can you tell us about their New Milestones project that you worked on?

MF: Yes, this was in the Tone valley in Somerset, and I was to make sculptures there that were in keeping with the landscape, not just visually but also historically. In this particular valley were the remains of a dismantled viaduct, a Brunel viaduct. It had been 100 feet, and when it was dismantled parts of it fell to the ground and embedded themselves there. I unearthed a five foot metal cross that had only had one inch of itself showing above the ground, and I used this in one of the sculptures. I cut a hazel tree back to about four feet in height, then sunk the metal into it. The hazel shoots will grow round the metal and eventually entomb it, and in future years you'll have the mystery, if you like, of how this metal got inside the tree. As a child when walking through the woods I'd quite often find metal that trees had grown round. They also grow through fences, on the side of cricket pitches for instance, or over barbed wire. So this harks back again to childhood, where I've seen these images and am now in a position to make them for myself. And

as a backdrop to this sculpture I used a huge alder tree that had four different trunks. They were about 70 feet high so everything else looks quite small, and the sculpture doesn't impinge on the landscape. It's a very gentle sculpture, a nice place to sit and contemplate the little river that runs through, and the birds, and the gnats which bite you to death, and the ducks on the River Tone nearby.

In 1987, Peter Randall Page was asked to make a sculpture for European Year of the Environment. It was commissioned for a new shopping development outside Basingstoke. The commission was an opportunity to bring to the attention of a large audience the fact that many species of living things are in danger.

'The issues are so important; I wanted to choose a theme which would draw people in. Initially I thought of using extinct species, but that gave no quality of hope, only despair. So I looked to see what species were endangered or in serious decline in Britain. The list was depressingly long.'

Peter chose a seed-pod from the spindle tree, a chrysalis of a swallowtail butterfly, and a shell of one of the two species of land snail which spiral anti-clockwise, both of which are endangered.

'I wanted the work to be still and quiet in mood, like life in a dormant or contained form. Each subject has a different kind of symmetry, and way of growing. Each is a vessel for life.

The natural forms were a starting point, and the sculpture developed and changed during the making.

'Here are things that are small and humble, the sort of things you might easily put your foot on, that might not be noticed if they disappeared. But once extinct, that's it! They are gone forever.'

The carvings are quite large, up to six feet in length; tiny objects on a monumental scale. Peter used Kilkenny limestone, a hard stone which takes a high finish. It was four months of intensive work with two assistants, working long days and physically very demanding.

The theme which unites most of Peter's work over the past five years is ecology.

'My work has always been more to do with my relationship with the world than a statement about art. For me, both (ecology and carving) share the idea of reconciliation between self and other, an ability to be the bit of creation that can stand back and look at itself, as well as being part of all the rest'.

from 'Celebration of Nature' by Malcolm Miles, *Resurgence magazine*, May/June 1989

After that summer, after being friends with Won-a-nee and her young, I never killed another otter. I had an otter cape for my shoulders, which I used until it wore out, but never again did I make a new one. Nor did I ever kill another cormorant for its beautiful feathers, though they have long, thin necks and make ugly sounds when they talk to each other. Nor did I kill seals for their sinews, using instead kelp to bind the things that needed it. Nor did I kill another wild dog, nor did I try to spear another sea elephant.

Ulape would have laughed at me, and others would have laughed, too – my father most of all. Yet this is the way I felt about the animals who had become my friends and those who had not, but in time could be. If Ulape and my father had come back and laughed, and all the others had come back and laughed, still I would have felt the same way, for animals and birds are like people, too, though they do not talk the same or do the same things. Without them the earth would be an unhappy place.

from *Island of the Blue Dolphins* by Scott O'Dell

The Hunter

The hunter stopped dead in his tracks
Weighing up the moon, the frozen pines,
The bits of white paper that would lead him back,
With nothing but an arrow in his mind.

Medbh McGuckian

Haiku

Wilder cats are nice.
They do not miaow they roar.
That's why I like them.

James Younger
Oakridge Junior School

Sealsong

Around me, seas
stretch endlessly;
above me, sky.
A space to breathe,
a place to swim;
to pace the days
by moon or sun.
A place that time
had kept from man;

no place to die.

Judith Nicholls

Beside the Seaside

Oh I do like to be beside the seaside,
Oh I do like to be beside the sea,
I do like to walk along the sewage pipe
Where the sand's got lumps
and the air smells ripe.
I do wish the sea would give the beach a wipe
Beside the seaside,
Beside the sea.

Oh I do like to walk beside the seaside,
Oh I do like to walk beside the sea,
I do like to see just what the tide's brought in
A plastic bag or two
And a rusty tin,
A long dead fish with a ghastly grin
Beside the seaside,
Beside the sea.

Oh I do like to paddle by the seaside,
I do like to paddle in the sea,
The sea's so dirty that no-one knows
What is oozing stickily
Around their toes.
You'll have a lovely time if you hold your nose
Beside the seaside,
Beside the sea.

David Orme

TUSK FORCE

The selling of ivory is against the law from this week, the latest move in the battle to protect the mighty elephant from being wiped out by poachers.

The ban affects both ivory from the tusks of newly slaughtered elephants, and old ivory, which may have been stockpiled by merchants waiting for the price to go up.

The African elephant population has dropped dramatically over the last 20 years because of poaching for ivory.

Early Times, 18 January 1990

Elephant

Elephant, death-bringer!
Elephant, spirit of the bush!
  With his one hand he brings two trees to the ground.
If he had two hands, he would tear the sky like an
  old rag.
Spirit who eats dog!
Spirit who eats ram!
Spirit who eats palm-fruit, thorns and all!
With four pestle-legs he flattens the grass,
Where he walks, the grass cannot stand again.
An elephant is no load for an old man –
Not even for a young man!

Yoruba, Nigeria

Jumbo Proverb Haiku

If you belittle
the elephant, prepare for
jumbo to squash you.

Please Save the Porcupine

In our school Miss Meacher
Is Cookery Teacher.
She says that to dine
Upon porcupine
Must quill the poor creature.

Debjani Chatterjee

No One Wants to be a Handbag

A crocodile
Will rarely smile
She knows your plans are drastic

She will save her skin
With a mirthless grin
And suggest you use some plastic

Trevor Millum

Frogs are killed to eat.
Why have frogs' legs, it's thick.
They belong in ponds.

Matthew Roughton
The Vyne School

49

Mr MIDDLETON says:

> Sharpen the edge of your spade.
> Don't take too much at a time.
> Digging is what you make it.

Mr MIDDLETON says:

> Never allow a weed to flower.
> Weeds mean work. Catch them young.
> Keep your tools clean and bright.

Mr MIDDLETON says:

> Plants are cleverer than we are.
> They make their own food, and ours too.
> Plant the best; it pays.

Mr MIDDLETON says:

> Grass needs care like other plants.
> A stake in time saves a plant in grime.
> I like to see a nice row of peas.

Mr MIDDLETON says:

> If onions fail you, try shallots.
> Give everything room to grow.
> Be prepared for pests and get there first.

Mr MIDDLETON says:

> Soil is the basis of life: take care of it.

Sue Stewart

Song of the Open Road

I think that I shall never see
A billboard lovely as a tree.
Perhaps, unless the billboards fall,
I'll never see a tree at all.

Ogden Nash

Sunday 31st . . . . I found a strawberry blossom in a rock. The little slender flower had more courage than the green leaves, for they were but half expanded and half grown, but the blossom was spread full out. I uprooted it rashly, and I felt as if I had been committing an outrage, so I planted it again. It will have a stormy life of it, but let it live if it can.

from *The Grasmere Journals*, January 1802,
by Dorothy Wordsworth

The Fir-Tree and the Bramble

A Fir-tree was one day boasting itself to a Bramble. 'You are of no use at all; but how could barns and houses be built without me? ' 'Good sir,' said the Bramble, 'when the woodmen come here with their axes and saws, what would you give to be a Bramble and not a Fir?'

A humble lot in security is better than the dangers that encompass the high and haughty.

Æsop's Fables

It is illegal to dig up any wild plant unless you have permission to do so from the person who owns the land it is growing on. It is also illegal to pick certain rare flowers. Many wild plants that were once common are now rare, partly because people have picked so many of them.

If you pick wild flowers, they will die, but if you leave them where they are, you will be able to go and look at them again and again, and so will other people.

from *The Usborne Spotter's Guide to Woodland Life*

51

Airy Hall Iconography

The Tamarind hangs its head,
stings the eyes with its breath.

The Mango traps the sun by degrees,
transforms its rays into ambrosia.

The Coconut's perfect seal lets in rain,
bends with solid milk and honey.

The Guava is its own harvest,
each seed bound in fleshy juice.

The Guinep's translucence is all yours
if you skin its lips, chew its seed for the raw.

The Stinking-toe might be lopped off a stale foot,
on the tongue it does an about-turn: myrrh.

The Paw-paw runs a feather along your nose,
you want it to stop, you want more.

The Sour-sop's veneer is the wasp
treading air at the vaulted honeycomb.

The Sapadilla ducks you twice in frankincense,
you are fished out fighting to go down a third time.

Fred D'Aguiar

Bamboozled!

A polar bear just loves an icy landscape,
The eagle likes a mountain with a view;
A whale demands an oceanful of water . . .
All *I* want is a thicket of BAMBOO!

The magpie gathers sticks and straw for nesting,
For a woodlouse some rotting bark will do;
The rabbit digs her home beneath the forest . . .
For *mine* I just need old stalks of BAMBOO!

Some tasty mouse is buzzard's choice for dinner
A field of grass is what a cow will chew;
Koalas can't resist their eucalyptus . . .
All *I* need is a bunch of ripe BAMBOO!

> *Please!*

> *Judith Nicholls*

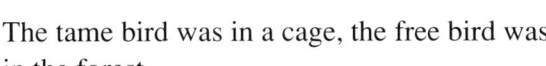

The tame bird was in a cage, the free bird was in the forest.

They met when the time came, it was a decree of fate.

The free bird cries, 'O my love, let us fly to wood.'

The cage bird whispers, 'Come hither, let us both live in the cage.'

Says the free bird, 'Among bars, where is there room to spread one's wings?'

'Alas,' cries the cage bird, 'I should not know where to sit perched in the sky.'

The free bird cries, 'My darling, sing the songs of the woodlands.'

The cage bird says, 'Sit by my side, I'll teach you the speech of the learned.'

The forest bird cries, 'No, ah no! songs can never be taught.'

The cage bird says, 'Alas for me, I know not the songs of the woodlands.'

Their love is intense with longing, but they never can fly wing to wing.

Through the bars of the cage they look, and vain is their wish to know each other.

They flutter their wings in yearning, and sing, 'Come closer, my love!'

The free bird cries, 'It cannot be, I fear the closed doors of the cage.'

The cage bird whispers, 'Alas, my wings are powerless and dead.'

from *The Gardener* by Rabindranath Tagore

Activities

Class dicussion

Read the interview with sculptor Michael Fairfax. What other materials could you use in a sculpture? Suggest as many as you can – for instance ice, newspapers, rope, iron, eggshells, glass. Discuss the special qualities each material has and how to make the best use of them.

Read the extract from Scott O'Dell's *Island of the Blue Dolphins*. If you were stranded on a deserted island, would you kill animals, birds or fish for any of the following reasons:

(i)   to protect yourself
(ii) to make feather capes or tooth necklaces
(iii) to use their skins to keep you warm
(iv) to eat?

Group activities

In groups of four, act out the 'Song of the Animal World'. Decide who will be the soloist, the fish, the bird and the monkey. Then all four of you join in the chorus of 'Hip! Viss! Gnan!' (These sounds represent the movements of the animals, not the noises they make.)

Then, using 'Song of the Animal World' as a model, make up your own song, with a different subject. For example, Song of the city/School song/Song of friends.

Read again Fred D' Aguiar's 'Airy Hall Iconography'. Then write your own mouthwatering poem, this time using more familiar fruits: apples, bananas, oranges, pears, grapefruit, peaches, cherries, grapes. Write two lines for each fruit, then put the lines together. Bring in more exotic fruits if you like, but only if you know them well.

Pair activities

Judith Nicholls says of her poem 'Sealsong':

'The seal that started this poem was a Monk Seal from the clear and beautiful waters of Hawaii; it *seemed* to be one of the most unlikely places in the world for such a creature to be in danger . . .

All my poems go through many drafts; in this one I spent a long time working on the different 'echoes'/near-rhymes inside the lines (moon/sun/man; swim/time; pace/days; seas/breathe . . .) leading up to the simple plea of the last line.'

Make a list of near-rhymes: see how many you can think of. Then use them to help you make a poem.

 Read Trevor Millum's 'Meadow Avenue'. The poet's left out all adjectives and adverbs: this is what makes it so direct. Write a short poem together, doing the same thing: if one of you spots an adjective or adverb, cross it out!

Individual writing

Read again 'Jumbo Proverb Haiku' by Debjani Chatterjee. Then see if you can make up some proverbs. Don't worry about writing them in the haiku style, but remember they need to be short and to the point.

Read 'Mr Middleton Says' on page 50. This is a 'found' poem, which means that every line was found in a book and rearranged by the poet into a poem. Using a book, newspaper or comic, copy out any lines that you especially like, then when you have about 15 lines see how you can best 'arrange' them into a poem. Change a word here or there if it helps the poem. Poems can be 'found' in other ways, too: tannoy announcements, overheard conversations, tombstones, letters, school reports, advertisements, snippets of radio talk, shouts at the fruit'n'veg market. Practise finding poems in unusual places.

Read the extract from Dorothy Wordsworth's journals. Imagine you're a gardener, looking after a small patch of land: write your diary for the week.

Using the Æsop's Fable as a model, write a fable on a green theme. Remember to find a good punch line!

Edna Eglinton says that her poem 'Riverside Cabaret' came from:

'the surprise discovery, during a lunch-time break in the middle of a busy day in a city office, of a secluded spot by a stream, close to a main road but shielded from it by trees and bushes.'

Imagine that you found a natural spot like this in the middle of a city: a patch of nettles full of butterflies, for instance, or a pond with frogs. Write a short story about it, remembering to give as much detail as possible. It can be a big discovery, or a little one: perhaps there's a real place you've found that you can write about.

Extension

Following on from the class discussion, make a series of sculptures using your chosen material. You can mix materials if you like, to bring out the difference between them – for instance, feather and stone, leaf and glass. Your sculptures can be upright, leaning against a wall, flat on the ground, or hanging in mid-air. If they're outdoor sculptures, they can move with the wind, melt under the sun. Experiment!

Or start a journal, recording each day the good and the bad things you notice about your environment.

Airwaves

Mother Parrot's Advice to her Children

Never get up till the sun gets up,
Or the mists will give you a cold,
And a parrot whose lungs have once been touched
Will never live to be old.

Never eat plums that are not quite ripe,
For perhaps they will give you a pain;
And never dispute what the hornbill says,
Or you'll never dispute again.

Never despise the power of speech;
Learn every word as it comes,
For this is the pride of the parrot race,
That it speaks in a thousand tongues.

Never stay up when the sun goes down,
But sleep in your own home bed,
And if you've been good, as a parrot should,
You will dream that your tail is red.

A K Nyabongo
Ganda, trans.

Leaving

Geese migrate
in celebration or routine,
elongated necks forward,
defining their destination
as webbed feet are folded back.
Journeys are slow,
slow as the copse they leave.
A contradiction, I think,
– the geese and trees –
one has freedom for comic motion,
exhaling an alarming din;
the other grows deeper into its silence.

Again, a grey flapping and suspended glide,
a cartoon animation
and a leaving . . .

Matthew Day
Heathfield School

Song

I had a dove and the sweet dove died;
    And I have thought it died of grieving.

O, what could it grieve for? Its feet were tied,
    With a silken thread of my own hand's weaving.
Sweet little red feet! why would you die –
Why should you leave me, sweet bird! why?
You lived alone on the forest-tree,
Why, pretty thing, could you not live with me?
I kissed you oft and gave you white peas;
Why not live sweetly, as in the green trees?

John Keats

Off the sharp point
Of a fisherman's arrow
I heard the cry
Of a wild cuckoo.

Where the cuckoo's voice
Glided into the sea
Shooting across the sky,
I found an island.

In the temple of Suma,
Under the shade of a tree,
I thought I had heard
An ancient flute on the march.

Matsuo Bashō

Haiku

The doves in the sky
flutter like crumpled paper
wheeling with the rooks.

Matthew Cousens
Shaw House School

Mama Dot's Treatise

Mosquitoes
Are the fattest
Inhabitants
Of this republic.

They suck our blood
From the cradle
And flaunt it
Like a fat wallet.

They form dark
Haloes; we spend
Our outdoors
Dodging sainthood.

They force us
Into an all-night
Purdah of nets
Against them.

O to stop them
Milking us
Till we are bait
For worms;

Worms that don't
Know which way
To turn and will
Inherit the earth.

Fred D'Aguiar

Going to Guyana

More than any South American Dictator
or any Death Squads, Secret Police or Juntas
what I'm afraid of more than anything
is the terrible malevolent Marabuntas . . .

they're huge wasps and they come at you
like not-too-well-intentioned fighter planes
swooping in to attack at all angles,
causing hideous mental and physical pains!

When Marabuntas are out, you don't hang about!
You don't linger!
Because each one's as big as a person's finger!

Gavin Ewart

* *Guyana is in South America, next to Brazil.*
 A 'junta' is a self-elected committee of
 people devoted to one political end. If you're
 Spanish you pronounce it 'hoon-tah'.

The Fly

Little Fly,
Thy summer's play
My thoughtless hand
Has brush'd away.

Am not I
A fly like thee?
Or art not thou
A man like me?

For I dance
And drink & sing,
Till some blind hand
Shall brush my wing.

If thought is life
And strength & breath,
And the want
Of thought is death,

Then am I
A happy fly
If I live
Or if I die.

William Blake

To Be Or Not To Be

I sometimes think I'd rather crow
And be a rooster than to roost
And be a crow. But I dunno.

A rooster he can roost also,
Which don't seem fair when crows can't crow.
Which may help, some. Still I dunno.

Crows should be glad of one thing, though;
Nobody thinks of eating crow,
While roosters they are good enough
For anyone unless they're tough.

There are lots of tough old roosters though,
And anyway a crow can't crow,
So mebby roosters stand more show.
It looks that way. But I dunno.

Anon

Sky High Sailor

High sky sailor
broken on the stones,
wears a wreath of maggots
on heather speared
           – with bones.

Sky high sailor
musk white eyes
feathers
limp
as dusters
breast a beat
of flies.
Sky land sailor
feasting highland fate
feeding on a cragside
feeding
mountain bait.

          Islay eagle
           see it die.
Seven foot deadspan.
         Once
              flew
                 high.

Peter Dixon

*This poem was written as a
'protest' about the poisoning of
eagles in Scotland*

The symbolism has not gone unnoticed in a stand-off over a pair of protected bald eagles which have decided to build a nest in a wood in Florida and have thus delayed, and may even prevent, the construction of a hazardous waste plant on an adjacent 86 acre site. 'I can't say the property can't be developed,' says a state wild-life official, 'but if you harass the eagles, you're going to jail.'

The Daily Mail, 3 January 1990

Flowers were plentiful that spring because of the winter's heavy rains. The dunes were covered with mats of sand flowers, which are red and have tiny eyes that are sometimes pink and sometimes white. Yuccas grew tall among the rocks of the ravine. Their heads were clustered with curly globes no larger than pebbles and the colour of the sun when it rises. Lupins grew where the springs ran. From the sunny cliffs, in crevices where no one would think anything could grow, sprang the little red and yellow fountains of the comul bush.

Birds were plentiful, too. There were many hummers which can stand still in the air and look like bits of polished stone and have long tongues to sip honey with. There were blue jays, which are very quarrelsome birds, and black-and-white peckers that pecked holes in the yucca stalks and the poles of my roof, even in the whale bones of the fence. Red-winged blackbirds also came flying out of the south, and flocks of crows, and a bird with a yellow body and a scarlet head, which I had never seen before.

A pair of these birds made a nest in a stunted tree near my house. It was made from strings of the yucca bush and had a small opening at the top and hung down like a pouch. The mother laid two speckled eggs which she and her mate took turns sitting on. After the eggs hatched, I put shreds of abalone under the tree and these she fed her young.

The young birds were not like their mother and father, being grey and very ugly, but anyway, I took them from the nest and put them in a small cage that I made of reeds. So later in the spring, when all the birds except the crows left the island and flew off to the north, I had these two for friends.

continued

They soon grew beautiful feathers like those of their parents and began to make the same sound, which was *reep, reep*. But it was soft and clear and much sweeter than the cries of the gulls or the crows or the talk of the pelicans which sounds like the quarrelling of toothless old men.

Before summer came the cage was too small for my two birds, but instead of building a larger one, I cut the tips of their wings, one wing of each, so they could not fly away, and let them loose in the house. By the time their wings had grown out, they had learned to take food from my hand. They would jump down from the roof and perch on my arm and beg, making their *reep, reep* sound.

When their wings began to feather out, I cut them again. This time I let them loose in the yard, where they hopped around hunting food, perching on Rontu who by now had gotten used to them. The next time they feathered out, I did not trim their wings, but they never flew farther away than the ravine and would always come back at night to sleep and, no matter how much they had eaten, to ask for food.

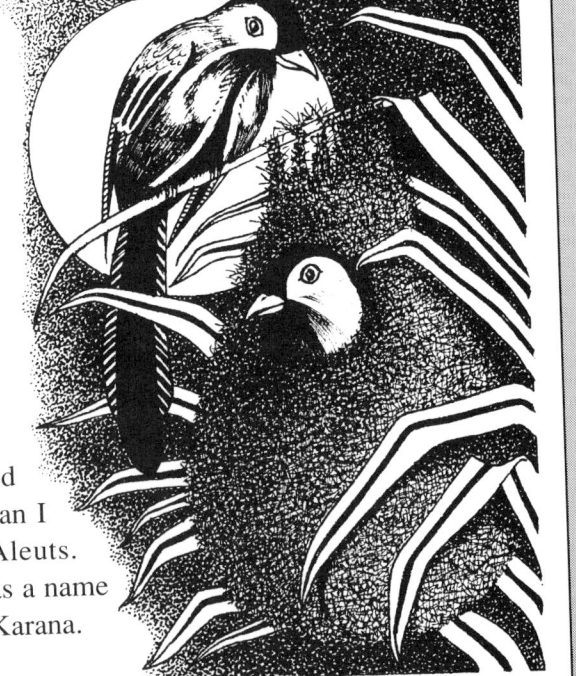

One, because he was larger, I called Tainor. I named him after a young man I liked who had been killed by the Aleuts. The other was called Lurai, which was a name I wished I had been called instead of Karana.

from *Island of the Blue Dolphins* by Scott O'Dell

A Quiet Day

The speck in the field's eye
Is the high hawk trawling his shadow.
His full wings say: to be hawk is sufficient.

The frog likes his silence;
Switches off fly's whine in mid-air.
His blink says: to be frog is good.

And starling, like a sewing machine
Stitches hedge to field and unpicks a worm.
His frown says: to be starling is important.

I lack their confidence,
Never sure that, in the end,
My own acts say: to be man is best.

Nigel Forde

The Thrush

Though all I wanted was to hear him sing
birds grow uneasy when we come too close
my presence made him flinch and take to wing

his voice had held the freshening power of spring
a spiral that continually rose
all I had wanted was to hear him sing

but birds well know the dangers that we bring
that men, since shame began, have been their foes
my presence made him flinch and take to wing

his song had seemed the key to everything
that runs or flies, that climbs and spreads and grows
all I had wanted was to hear him sing

like spools of light I heard his gracecalls ring
but I was not the audience he chose
my presence made him flinch and take to wing

silenced, he fled, and left his branch to swing
beyond my hearing now his message goes
though all I wanted was to hear him sing
my presence made him flinch and take to wing

Joan Aiken

Friday June 25th . . . . I looked up at my Swallow's nest and it was gone. It had fallen down. Poor little creatures they could not themselves be more distressed than I was. I went upstairs to look at the Ruins. They lay in a large heap upon the window ledge; these Swallows had been ten days employed in building this nest, and it seemed to be almost finished. I had watched them early in the morning, in the day many and many a time and in the evenings when it was almost dark I had seen them sitting together side by side in their unfinished nest both morning and night. When they first came about the window they used to hang against the panes, with their white Bellies and their forked tails looking like fish, but then they fluttered and sang their own little twittering song.

from *The Grasmere Journals*, June 1802,
by Dorothy Wordsworth

'Race you to the donkey field!' he yelled, and she took up his challenge and broke into a loose run as the path flattened and swung into the shelter of overhanging trees. He stumbled after her, his shoes slapping the hard earth, watching the swing of her yellow hair. 'Can't make it. I'm a dead man.' He nursed a stitch that bent him sideways. He watched Elaine as she clambered up the leaning stone wall that surrounded the donkey field. She held herself there, motionless, with her hand lifted to shield her eyes. He limped up to her, drawing in his breath and groaning so that she wouldn't laugh at him for losing the race, but she swung her arm behind her in a warning gesture, and he pulled himself up beside her and sat with his legs straddling the hump of the wall; silent.

He saw immediately what she was looking at. A large white bird moved across the field towards them; a bird with a broad heavy head and wide blunt wings. It swung upwards, its great wings driving it like a swimmer through still water, and it drifted, bullet-headed, a huge silent moth, lifting itself soundlessly, while the air hung quiet around it. In the middle of the field the donkeys pressed and nudged each other, flicking their ears idly, unconscious of the dark shadow gliding over them.

'What is it?'

'It's an owl,' said Elaine softly. She couldn't take her eyes off it.

Steven slid off the wall and lay with the long grass criss-crossed over him. 'But owls are night birds.' He followed the slow flight of the bird quartering the field. With a last wide sweep that swung it high above their heads it left the field and floated across the wide valley, and was lost among the dark trees that shadowed the river on the far side; miles away.

continued

Elaine slid down beside him and they trudged across the field. Steven pointed out some deep trenches that had been cut across the far end. They stretched out in a line from the end of the housing estate to the village lane, and they seemed to be huge squares dug into the soil. They walked slowly round them.

'What d'you think these are?' Steven asked. 'Why should someone dig up the donkey field?'

'I dunno,' said Elaine. 'Donkeys had better watch it, or they'll drop in.'

They both giggled.

'Come on,' said Steven. 'Let's ask Mr Dyson about that bird.'

He raced away from her, and she followed him slowly, her mind on the great white bird with sunlight like cream across its back . . . . . .

. . . . When the letter came from the council telling them that the cottages in their lane were to be demolished to make way for the new development Mrs Dyson hid it in fear from her husband. She spent hours in her garden, pulling up weeds uselessly. 'It's coming, it's coming,' she said to herself. 'There's no stopping cities.' They'd have a modern house with proper facilities. They'd be surrounded. It would make a change. It would break the old man's heart.

The last day in September was brilliantly sunny. Steven and Elaine had nothing to do, and decided to go down to the river together. Steven was shy about asking Elaine to come with him now. They picnicked there and she lay back, catching a last suntan, while Steven skimmed pebbles on the water and watched the wagtails and dippers bobbing on the stony banks. They'd come the long way because that would bring them back on their favourite walk past

the farm with the goats and eventually, up the long hill to the donkey field. They didn't mention the owl to each other. He belonged to a part of the summer that was past.

'Race you to the donkey field!' he challenged as they panted up the slope.

'Not the donkey field now!' she reminded him. 'Housing estate.'

They scrambled up the steep slope and Elaine swung along the path, with Steven close behind her, and as they clambered up the stone wall there it was again; the white owl, in the full brilliance of the late afternoon: Barney. Low over the grass, and below them, with its broad strong head and its pale soft back, quartering the field of half-grown houses with slow lifts of its wings. There was no other movement in the field. Not a sound.

continued

Elaine and Steven stood, breathless, on the wall, following Barney's route across the field, and suddenly Steven's eyes were stopped by an unfamiliar bundle in the grass, a twist of drab colour, humped at an angle. He turned sharply to Elaine and she smiled and nodded and laid her hand on his arm. Mr Dyson, lying in the long grass at the side of the field, raised his arm slowly as if in a salute, and rested his hand as a shield above his eyes, watching the movements of the daylight owl.

Steven thought of the old man dragging himself to the front of his shop; his slow unsteady shuffle. It must have taken him hours to get himself down the lane, past the little school, through all the rubble of the building site and across the rough grass to where he lay now, folded in a corner of the field. He forgot to watch Barney, and when he looked again the bird was making its last circle of the field. It rose higher and higher, right into the line of the sun, nearly blinding him, and then it drifted out across the valley to its dark shelter. Steven knew he would never see it again.

from *Owls are Night Birds* by Berlie Doherty

Christopher

Christopher was a light boy who learned to fly.
With the feathers of gulls he went high in the sky.
It was hot up there,
sun had burned through.
Hard to breathe up there,
sky wasn't blue.
And the scraps of spaceships floating by.
Christopher didn't like to be in the sky.

Christopher came down in the Black Forest.
The wild boars thought him a feathered tourist.
It was a shock in there,
pine trees dying.
Didn't anyone care?
Who was trying?
And the sour water in the mountain stream.
Christopher swallowed an echoey scream.

Christopher took to the grey sky again.
He floated over the walking insane.
Beyond them, the sea.
Behind, a river.
Couldn't they see
they had to live here?
And the choking clouds from their cars.
Christopher wished he could fly to the stars.

Matthew Sweeney

The Teabag

There's a hole in the teabag
Where the sun gets in,
It's far too strong
And it ruins our skin.

CFC's and poisonous gases,
Jason's spray and Mr Sheen
Will destroy the earth,
So keep it clean.

The greenhouse effect
Will make us steam,
Stitch up the teabag
And keep the world green.

You've heard the song,
You've heard me saying
Ban spray cans
Or you'll be paying.

Edward Wall
Chawton C E (Controlled) Primary School

Haiku

Hairspray makes a cloud
which floats to the atmosphere,
killing us with holes.

Clare Emery
The Vyne School

Activities

Class discussion

Read the *Daily Mail* piece about the eagles nesting in a wood in Florida. Why is this seen as 'symbolic'? Do you think the eagles had an instinct for what they were doing – apart from the usual nest-building instinct? Or was it just chance?

Talk about what makes an 'intelligent' bird, fish, animal or mammal. Here are some you might like to start with: dolphin, salmon, magpie, elephant, bee, snake, woodpecker, cat, tortoise, ant, squirrel, whale, monkey, bat, spider, hedgehog.

Not all creatures are friendly! Read 'Going to Guyana' by Gavin Ewart. Are there any other dangerous or annoying creatures you know about? What is it that makes these creatures attack human beings? For instance, would a mosquito and a mother eagle attack for the same reason?

Group activities

Discuss some of the difficult poems in this section, such as 'Mama Dot's Treatise,' 'The Fly' 'A Quiet Day' and 'Leaving'. Do you understand all the words, and the way they're arranged (the 'syntax')? Use dictionaries to help you.

The poem 'The Thrush' by Joan Aiken is written in the form of a 'villanelle'. Look closely at the poem. Can you see what the form is? Make out a set of guidelines for writing a villanelle.
There's another villanelle in the *Big world, little world* section: perhaps you can find it.

Pair activities

Read the extract from *Island of the Blue Dolphins* by Scott O'Dell, and compare it with the extract from *The Gardener* by Tagore in the *Songs of the wild* section. Talk about the different views expressed. Then, making up your own green theme, each write about it from a different point of view. For instance, should a butterfly sanctuary in a deprived inner city area be destroyed to make room for an adventure playground?

Read the poem 'To Be Or Not To Be' on page 61. Decide on an animal you both like. Then write alternate stanzas of a poem, one writing about the good things in your animal's life, the other about the bad.

Individual writing

 Read again the poem 'Mother Parrot's Advice to her Children' by A K Nyabongo. Write a poem about another bird or animal giving her offspring advice: for example, mouse, earwig, sparrow, deer, spider, hawk.

 Nigel Forde says of his poem 'A Quiet Day':

'I wanted to draw a tiny portrait of each creature in as short a time as possible; to pick out the really froggy aspects of the frog, what was especially hawk-like about the hawk. If you had written it what would you have picked out?'

Study the form of the poem, particularly the last line of each stanza. Following the same form, write a poem about your favourite birds.

 Peter Dixon wrote his 'Sky High Sailor' poem as a protest about the poisoning of eagles in Scotland. This is a 'elegy', a poem of mourning. Write your own elegy for a bird, fish or mammal injured or poisoned by human beings.

 Read again the poem 'Christopher' by Matthew Sweeney. If you could fly, how would you use this gift? After making notes, write it up as a story.

 Read the extract from *Owls are Night Birds* by Berlie Doherty. Other winged creatures come out only, or mainly, at night. Can you think of any? Imagine you are one of them, and you go exploring in the daytime. Write your diary for the day.

Extension

Set up a bird register for the school, with a written description of each bird, its habitats and habits, and its song. Then make a painting of each bird to accompany the register. Include birds from other countries if you know them well enough.

What time is it?

Four Quarters

Spring
The wind has moved West
It shifted last night
I woke this morning
The garden was white
The raven last evening
Called winter home
But this morning the blackbird
And she was gone.

Summer
The wind has gone South
I don't recall when
I slept one moment
The garden turned green
The blackbird last evening
Sang it was spring
But this morning the cuckoo
And she was gone.

Autumn
The wind has moved East
The year's growing old
I caught her whisper
The garden turned gold
The cuckoo last evening
Called summer in
But this morning the robin
And she was gone.

Winter
The wind has moved North
Its teeth are laid bare
I searched the garden
Found nobody there
The robin last evening
Cheeped autumn's song
But this morning the raven
And she has gone.

John Moat

May Evening

Three rabbits thread a fence.
A young ram stamps twice,
arches his neck. I ought to
lend him a mirror.

Four Charolais calves,
all angles and soft white suede,
twitch the yellow stapled ear tags
that match their mothers'.

Cracked cough of a heron
from the larch tops.
Snap of tiny trout
leaping for gnats.

Patricia Pogson

English Summer

Hold on a minute!
Someone has pinched
the sun.

I can tell, because
there is a light mark
where it used to hang

which looks most unsightly.
Besides, Summer should be hot.
If I remember rightly.

Carol Ann Duffy

That Flower

Summer, autumn, winter, spring,
It swells in my head, always blossoming

I mean the artichoke's bright flower,
I feel it growing hour by hour

I saw it in a field beside
The brimmimg sea, the racing tides

A purple crown it was, a crest
Of colour worn for happiness

Purple against the plant's grey fist
Purple against the sea's blue mist

Purple against the weight of sorrow
Here today and here tomorrow

The artichoke, I mean – its flower
That grows in my head through sun and showers

Past autumn, winter, spring and summer
Waving its crest to every comer.

Lawrence Sail

The Last Forest

On a hill at the centre of the earth
Stood the last forest.
Everywhere else was barren plain.
People came from all over
To admire the phenomenon of trees growing.
Among these visitors were writers,
Who, more than anyone else there present,
Understood this miracle of a forest that continued to grow,
And in their worthy passion to describe it
For those too weak or stupid or poor or ill or old
To travel to the forest on the hill at the centre of the earth,
Little by little cut down the forest for pencils and paper.

Leo Aylen

The Tree-planter Laughs at Himself

At seventy I am still planting trees,
But let not my neighbours mock my folly.
From the beginning there has indeed been death,
But it is well that we have no fore-knowledge.

Yüan Mei

THE TREE MAN

Listen, here's a true story.

In France, about the time the father of your dad's father was a boy, in the mountains of the high Provence, in the southern part of the Drome, there was a place where the world had gone rotten. Nothing any longer grew; the houses had all fallen down. Only three people still lived there, and they had gone bitter as potatoes that have gone bitter in the sun. They hated each other. The only person who ever came visiting this high lonely place was the wind, and he liked it so little that he whistled straight through.

But then one day someone did come. He was a small man, and standing there in the sunlight of that lonely wild place he looked like a single lonely tree. He stood for a time and stared about him and then he went away.

Two days later he was back. He was walking a dog who was walking behind some sheep. Over his shoulder he carried a sack which may have been the heaviest sack that any man ever has carried. In the sack was a forest of trees, green trees in sunlight with a warm wind lingering in the leaves. Which isn't entirely true, but which like all riddles is truer than it first might appear. That sack was heavy with acorns.

The man's name was Monsieur Elzeard Bouffier. His wife had died and his son had died, and he'd decided to live on his own. But not entirely alone. Up in those lonely highlands he found a ruined cottage. And he moved in with his dog, and his sheep. His sheep? Well, I don't know about the sheep, but certainly he moved in with his acorns.

continued

Monsieur Bouffier settled down to a new way of life. Every evening, when he had penned his sheep, and he and his dog had shared a shepherd's stew, he would go to the sack and fetch a basin of acorns. Then he would examine them one by one, and the ones that were perfect he would put in a pile. When he had found a hundred perfect acorns . . . that was it, he'd go to bed. Next morning, early, he and his dog would lead the sheep out to graze on the lean upland grass. When they were content he would leave the dog in charge, and he, with his iron staff and his small leather bag, would climb to a special place on the mountain side.

With his staff he would drive a hole in the ground, and in the hole he would plant an acorn. Ninety-nine to go. He would plant acorn after acorn until he had planted one hundred acorns. Every day the same, a hundred acorns. Each day enough for a new little wood. Yes, but up there where nothing, not even the thin grass, seemed eager to grow, would an oak-tree ever grow?

No one visited the place, but far away, from time to time, people would pass by. They would look up at the dead deserted place and shudder and hurry on their way. But wait! One day some three years after Monsieur Bouffier began his new life, a traveller glanced at the distant wilderness, and then he looked again, and then he gave the wilderness a long hard look. There was one part different from the rest, a little area that appeared caught in a tender bluish light, as if there were a haze of bluey green, or a warm drifting of smoke. After a minute the traveller shrugged his shoulders. Perhaps it was a trick of the light. He hurried on.

You know what it was?

In three years Monsieur Bouffier had planted one hundred thousand acorns. Eighty thousand of these had never taken root. Yes, but twenty thousand had. Of these twenty thousand the mice and rats and the rabbits had eaten ten thousand. So that left only ten thousand. Only? There were ten thousand oak trees growing where there had been nothing growing before.

But Monsieur Bouffier had only just begun. The years, with their four-season tick, ticked by. And with each full tick Monsieur Bouffier planted another thirty thousand acorns.

Tick. Tick. Tick. Thirty, sixty, ninety thousand trees.

He planted beech trees with their gleaming silvery leaves that seemed to run like water in the wind. And birch trees in the hollows where water lay near the surface. One year he planted ten thousand maple trees, and they all died.

But from far away people began to see what was happening. A forest was appearing out of the wilderness, and no one understood why. It was a miracle. It was a freak of nature . . . Twenty-five years after Monsieur Bouffier began to plant, a man from the ministry, a forest warden, called on him. He told Monsieur Bouffier that Monsieur Bouffier probably didn't realise it but he was living in the only forest that had ever been known to grow entirely by itself. He imagined that Monsieur Bouffier didn't know anything about trees, let alone these unusual trees, and he told him to be careful about lighting fires in the open. Monsieur Bouffier said nothing. He was then seventy-five years old, and the forest was so large that he now had to walk twelve miles from his cottage to get to where there was room to plant more trees.

When the war came, there was a shortage of wood. Then up drove the men with the big saws and they started to fell the fine oak trees Monsieur Bouffier had planted forty years before. But the trees were so far from any road that the men found they couldn't shift the fallen wood, and they lost money and gave up. But Monsieur Bouffier knew nothing about all this: he was eighteen miles away . . . planting more trees.

By now Monsieur Bouffier had given up sheep and taken to keeping honey-bees for a living. The sheep couldn't keep pace with him when he walked twenty miles to plant trees, but bees . . . bees find their own way home.

When he was eighty-seven, Monsieur Bouffier was still planting trees. By then he had lived alone so long that he no longer spoke a single word. Maybe he had forgotton how to speak, or maybe he had learned from the trees that silence says all that needs to be said. He died peacefully when he was ninety.

Was he a madman? Had he ever spared a thought for anyone else? Well, you tell me. The wilderness he had come to half a century before had entirely changed. Even the air; that dry gusting wind had given way to a sweet, scent-laden breeze.

continued

A murmur like the sea came from the hillsides; it was a wind in the trees. And strangest of all, everywhere in that former wilderness there was now the clear miraculous sound of tumbling water. Even the climate had changed.

Within eight years of Monsieur Bouffier's death the whole region was flourishing. The ruins had been rebuilt, were once again well-kept farms. The old springs, fed by rain and snow stored by the tree-roots, were running again. Beside each farm was a maple copse, and a fountain spilling onto a carpet of fresh mint. Even villages were coming alive, and the countryside was full of business and laughter and the sound of kids playing. You remember the number of trees that took root in Monsieur Bouffier's first three years? That's right, ten thousand. Well now, eight years after his death, there were the same number of people living in that region . . . all of whom owed their happiness and their livelihood to Monsieur Bouffier. Hey! Now wait a minute! Didn't they also owe it to the trees?

So next time you come to an oak tree, look at it closely. Look at the size of it. Think how long it took to grow. If you see an acorn lying around, why not plant it . . . about three inches down in good earth, and if possible where there's plenty of light. As you do that think how many trees one man can plant in a lifetime, and remember there was a minute once when Monsieur Bouffier – yes, he too – had in the whole of his life planted only one acorn.

John Moat
This story, adapted as a performance piece from 'The Man Who Planted Trees' by Jean Giono, was commissioned by Cy Grant

Haiku

One leaf left, the oak
spreads bare arms. No nuts cluster
in its wooden web.

Hannah Kirby
Shaw House School

Haiku

The once green leaves fall
reluctantly to the ground.
Then the rain, tap . . . tap.

Elizabeth Dunne
Shaw House School

Tree in the Heart of the Void

The beginning was void. The first thing to be
formed in the heart of the void was a tree.
This first tree sprang out of a womb of energy,
and, emerging from its millions of buds, there
sprouted the whole of creation.

Maori creation myth

Wood

Root, bark, branch and leaves
are ancient monuments,
our living past.

Wooden capillaries
clatter their silhouettes
to form music.

They stand forward with pride
like natural soldiers
with no defence,

dominated by us.
Unthinking, we will lose
their knowledge, gone.

A hundred years of growth
is toppled, trees made weak,
memories lost.

We have nothing to gain.
A chair rots in the rain like
our wasteful minds.

Woodsmen with their chainsaw
leave wood a memory,
our past felled.

Blossom Wyson
Heathfield School

Atomic Courtesy

To smash the simple atom
All mankind was intent.
      Now any day
      The atom may
Return the compliment.

Ethel Jacobson

Five Haiku

Tea-leaf in my cup:
did you read your own future,
growing in China?

~

Rain surprises us
like commas, punctuating
summer's flummery.

~

Elderberries hang
like a bunch of purple keys
unlocking wine.

~

Clip the columbine:
air-borne castanets of seed
land like rattlesnakes.

~

In a blade of grass
is voice for green politics:
the tongue's cutting edge.

Sue Stewart

From the Hill

Just
at dusk
the moon
winks.
One
by one
where the light was
birds are.
From here
the village hardly is,
but snow says
the same thing
over and over again.
Below the stars
Me.
Below me,
At one breath,
the winter
goes
out.

Nigel Forde

Birdshooting Season

Birdshooting season the men
make marriages with their guns
My father's house turns macho
as from far the hunters gather

All night long contentless women
stir their brews: hot coffee
chocolata, cerassie
wrap pone and tie-leaf
for tomorrow's sport. Tonight
the men drink white rum neat.

In darkness shouldering
their packs, their guns, they leave

We stand quietly on the
doorstep shivering. Little boys
longing to grow up birdhunters too
Little girls whispering:

Fly Birds Fly.

Olive Senior

Bird

That day the bird hunted an empty, gleaming sky
and climbed and coiled and spun measures of joy,
half-sleeping in the sly wind way
above my friend and me. Oh,
its wings' wind-flick and fleche were free
and easy in the sun, and a whip's tip
tracing of pleasure its mute madrigal,
that I below watched it so tall
it could not fall save slow
down the slow day.

'What is it?' said my friend
'Yonder . . . .'
                        Hill and home patterned and curved
and frozen in the white round air
'Yes, there,' he said, 'I see it – '

                        Up

the steep sky till the eye
lidded from weight of sun on earth and wing!

'Watch this,' he said, bending for stones,
and my boy's throat grew tight with warning
to the bird that rode the feathered morning.

'Now there's a good shot, boy!' he said.
I was only ten then.
'If you see any more be sure to shout
but don't look at the sun too long,' he said,
'makes your eyes run.'

Dennis Scott

The Dry Season

The year is withering; the wind
Blows down the leaves;
Men stand under the eaves
And overhear the secrets
Of the cold dry wind,
Of the half-bare trees.

The grasses are tall and tinted,
Straw-gold hues of dryness,
And the contradicting awryness
Of the dusty roads a-scatter
With pools of colourful leaves,
With ghosts of the dreaming year.

And soon, soon the fires,
The fires will begin to burn,
The hawk will flutter and turn
On its wings and swoop for the mouse,
The dogs will run for the hare,
The hare for its little life.

Kwesi Brew

Friend

Do you remember
that wild stretch of land
with the lone tree guarding the point
from the sharp-tongued sea?

The fort we built out of branches
wrenched from the tree, is dead wood now.
The air that was thick with the whirr of
toetoe spears succumbs at last to the grey gull's wheel.

Oyster-studded roots
of the mangrove yield no finer feast
of silver-bellied eels, and sea-snails
cooked in a rusty can.

Allow me to mend the broken ends
of shared days:
but I wanted to say
that the tree we climbed
that gave food and drink
to youthful dreams, is no more.
Pursed to the lips her fine-edged
leaves made whistle – now stamp
no silken tracery on the cracked
clay floor.

Friend,
in this drear
dreamless time I clasp
your hand if only for reassurance
that all our jewelled fantasies were
real and wore splendid rags.

Perhaps the tree
will strike fresh roots again:
give soothing shade to a hurt and
troubled world.

Hone Tuwhare

After luncheon, accordingly, when the other two had settled themselves into the chimney-corner and had started a heated argument on the subject of *eels*, the Badger lighted a lantern and bade the Mole follow him. Crossing the hall, they passed down one of the principal tunnels, and the wavering light of the lantern gave glimpses on either side of rooms both large and small, some mere cupboards, others nearly as broad and imposing as Toad's dining-hall. A narrow passage at right angles led them into another corridor, and here the same thing was repeated. The Mole was staggered at the size, the extent, the ramifications of it all; at the length of the dim passages, the solid vaultings of the crammed store-chambers, the masonry everywhere, the pillars, the arches, the pavements. 'How on earth, Badger,' he said at last, 'did you ever find time and strength to do all this? It's astonishing!'

'It *would* be astonishing indeed,' said the Badger simply, 'if I *had* done it. But as a matter of fact I did none of it – only cleaned out the passages and chambers, as far as I had need of them. There's lots more of it, all round about. I see you don't understand, and I must explain it to you. Well, very long ago, on the spot where the Wild Wood waves now, before ever it had planted itself and grown up to what it now is, there was a city – a city of people, you know. Here, where we are standing, they lived, and walked, and talked, and slept, and carried on their business. Here they stabled their horses and feasted, from here they rode out to fight or drove out to trade. They were a powerful people, and rich, and great builders. They built to last, for they thought their city would last for ever.'

'But what has become of them all?' asked the Mole.

'Who can tell?' said the Badger. 'People come – they stay for a while, they flourish, they build – and they go. It is their way. But we remain. There were badgers here, I've been told, long before that same city ever came to be. And now there are badgers here again. We are an enduring lot, and we may move out for a time, but we wait, and are patient, and back we come. And so it will ever be.'

continued

'Well, and when they went at last, those people?' said the Mole.

'When they went,' continued the Badger, 'the strong winds and persistent rains took the matter in hand, patiently, ceaselessly, year after year. Perhaps we badgers too, in our small way, helped a little – who knows? It was all down, down, down, gradually – ruin and levelling and disappearance. Then it was all up, up up, gradually, as seeds grew to saplings, and saplings to forest trees, and bramble and fern came creeping in to help. Leaf-mould rose and obliterated, streams in their winter freshets brought sand and soil to clog and to cover, and in course of time our home was ready for us again, and we moved in. Up above us, on the surface, the same thing happened. Animals arrived, liked the look of the place, took up their quarters, settled down, spread, and flourished. They didn't bother themselves about the past – they never do; they're too busy. The place was a bit humpy and hillocky, naturally, and full of holes; but that was rather an advantage. And they don't bother about the future, either – the future when perhaps the people will move in again – for a time – as may very well be. The Wild Wood is pretty well populated by now; with all the usual lot, good, bad, and indifferent – I name no names. It takes all sorts to make a world. But I fancy you know something about them yourself by this time.'

'I do indeed,' said the Mole, with a slight shiver.

from *The Wind in the Willows* by Kenneth Grahame

The Old Tree Stump

The old stump
is all that remains
of an elm tree
felled years ago.
Now it's our garden seat
comfortably covered
with a moss cushion
upon which our cat
sleeps in the sun.

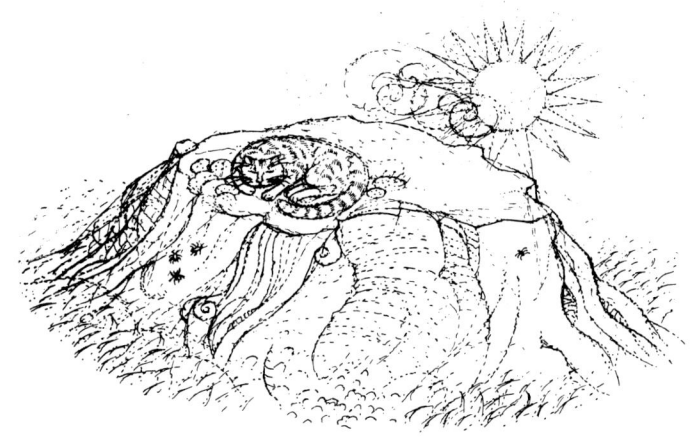

A dead stump?
Peel back the bark
and see scores of ants
swarming like Londoners
in the rush hour
or watch the woodlice
trundling like army tanks
to the front line
of some forgotten war.

And here's a centipede
plunging down a crack
like a potholer
exploring unknown caverns.
Later, when we've gone,
a thrush alights
and uses the stump as an anvil
upon which to smash
a land snail's shell.

It's a favourite spot
in our garden,
this old tree stump,
and – you know –
it's quite the best
place to sit
and sun yourself
on a sweltering day
in the middle of July.

Wes Magee

Activities

Class discussion

Nigel Forde says of his poem 'From the Hill':

'This poem tries to recapture the first time I realised that a split second can be full of all sorts of meanings and feelings. One moment it was evening and the next moment, though hardly anything seemed to have happened, it was definitely night.'

The world is always changing, and our lives with it. Perhaps something happened in your life that suddenly altered it: travel, a change in your family circumstances, making a new friend, changing schools, moving home. Or you might just have changed your outlook, seen things from another point of view. Share these moments of change with the class if you feel able to.

Read again the poem 'That Flower'. Lawrence Sail says of his poem:

'Sometimes you come across something that defeats time just by staying so bright in your mind and memory – even when it's something which, like a flower, is at the mercy of time.'

What sorts of things do you remember? Perhaps you loved a particular animal – a family pet, or a wild creature – which has since died. Does it live on in your imagination? Perhaps you saw something – a beautiful flower, or bird, or scene, which you will never forget. Or was it something you heard? Go over the five senses to see if they trigger any memories for you. Are there any particular memories – good or bad – that you'd be prepared to share with the class?

Group activities

In groups of four, read the song 'Four Quarters' by John Moat. Then each write a verse for one of the seasons, putting them all together to make a full song.

A musician put 'Four Quarters' to music, and now it's on record and cassette. If you are able to, draw up a musical score for your song, using a variety of musical instruments. Then perform it to the rest of the class.

Read the 'Five Haiku' on page 85. Can you work out what a 'haiku' is? Then can you spot the odd one out?

There are several haiku in this book: see how many you can find. Then, as a group, decide on a subject you'd like to write about, and each person contribute one haiku.

Pair activities

What will your village/town/city be like in 300 years? One of you write an optimistic view, the other a pessimistic one.

John Moat's story The Tree Man was originally broadcast on radio. Imagine that, at the end of his life, M Bouffier is interviewed about his life for a radio programme. Plan out the questions you would ask him, then improvise the interview.

Individual writing

Write a story about one of the memories you shared with the class earlier – or about any other memory of yours. Remember to use all the five senses in the story, and give as much detail as possible.

Study the form of 'From the Hill' by Nigel Forde. The poet has arranged the words in this way to make you read the poem slowly. How do you think this helps our understanding of the poem?
Write your own 'thin' poem, trying to get as much meaning into each short line as you can.

What does Olive Senior's poem 'Birdshooting Season' say about the difference between men and women? The poet was writing about her own childhood: do you think things have changed since then? Write a poem, based on an experience of yours, that shows either how alike, or how unalike, girls and boys are.

Read again the poem by Leo Aylen, 'The Last Forest'. Then write your own poem about the 'last' of something. Here are some suggestions: feather, raindrop, stone, claw, shell, bone, flame, whisker, tail.

Read the extract from *The Wind in the Willows* by Kenneth Grahame. Imagine that the Ministry of Transport is considering building a B road through the Wild Wood, to prevent overcrowding and accidents on the nearby A road. Write a letter *either* to the Ministry to protest at this, *or* to Badger, giving the Ministry's point of view.

Extension

Make an exhibition based on the subject of trees. Include poems, paintings, leaf prints and growth charts, and collect seeds or nuts. Make up an A – Z of trees, explaining such things as tree rings, bark, sap, deciduous. Collect fallen twigs to make a mobile, or fallen branches to make a bigger sculpted piece. Draw up a world map and pin tree badges on it to show which trees grow where. Include as many trees as you can, and from different countries.

John Moat says of his story *The Tree Man*:
'I came on Jean Giono's original version of this story when I was feeling the world was in a terrible mess, and that I could do nothing about it. Immediately I knew I was wrong. Even if I planted one tree, or one a year, or . . . so why don't you, or your class, or your school find a patch or bit of wasteland, and plant a tree, or a copse, or a wood and look after it, and watch it grow, and see what life comes to it, and from it, and hand it on to others to look after?'

If you have any pocket money, you could also write to the Woodland Trust, who will plant a tree in your name on one of their ten sites for £1. If your class can club together and collect as much as £25, you can then choose which of the sites your 25 trees are planted on. Or your teacher could write to the British Trust for Conservation Volunteers, which has many tree-planting schemes. The Trust works all over the country with local groups who want to plant trees in their own areas. Both these addresses are at the end of the book.

Big world, little world

Whose Anyway?

The forest is mine
   said the squirrel
No, it's mine said
   the woodpecker.
It's mine said the woodsman
   with his chainsaw.

The sea is mine
   said the whale
No, it's mine said
   the oyster and crab.
It's mine said the oil tanker
   spilling crude oil.

The land is mine
   said the lion
No, it's mine said
   the mouse and mole.
It's mine said the builder
   with concrete and glass.

The air is mine
   said the albatross
No, it's mine said
   the robin and wren.
It's mine said the aircraft
   jetting the sky.

The world is mine
   said the merchant
No, it's mine said
   the politician.
It's me cries the voice
   of the planet.

John Fairfax

World

I could not hope
to touch the sky
with my two arms.

Full moon

The glow and beauty of the stars
are nothing near the splendid moon
when in her roundness she burns silver
about the world.

Ceremony

Now the earth with many flowers
puts on her spring embroidery.

Sappho

The living planet
had the morning sky hiding the stars.

The dead planet
had no sky to hide the stars.

Lee Matthews
The Vyne School

Spring Clean

Clean up!
Roared the universe
This room
Is a disgrace!

And sadly muttering
Of course
A shamed flower
Hid its face.

John Mole

Fire and Ice

Some say the world will end in fire;
Some say in ice.
From what I've tasted of desire
I hold with those who favor fire.
But if it had to perish twice,
I think I know enough of hate
To know that for destruction ice
Is also great
And would suffice.

Robert Frost

MARK OF THE BEAST

GLOBAL WARMING led to the hurricane gale which caused the death of at least 50 people last week. The breakdown of the ozone layer, due, amongst other things, to the increased use of CFCs over the past decades, has led to global warming.

The earth cannot be protected from the sun's powerful rays and the earth's temperature increases. The temperature of the Southern Atlantic is between one and two degrees centigrade higher than it normally is at this time of year.

In contrast, the south-eastern states of America are experiencing one of their coldest winters.

The temperature contrast between the cold land and warmer than average sea creates the energy which caused the depression. This depression gathered force as it rushed across the Atlantic – then the winds of death hit Britain.

People were killed by falling trees or swirling debris, roads were blocked, commuters stranded and the Severn Bridge closed for only the third time in its history.

Insurance companies are devastated, with estimates standing at £1 billion for last week's freak winds. After the 1987 gale they had to pay out £1.3 billion.

In 1987, BBC weatherman Michael Fish dismissed predictions of a hurricane. The next day the worst hurricane on record hit the south of England; Sevenoaks in Kent became one oak. But this time Michael knew what was coming, and gave a special warning on Wednesday to his viewers.

As the ozone layer becomes more depleted we can expect more freak weather conditions. If the North Pole's ice caps continue to melt, then we can also expect flooding as the level of the sea rises. East Anglia will start to disappear. So the real beast involved is man. Our destruction of rainforests, our use of chemicals and our disregard for the equilibrium of nature have had much greater effect than we ever imagined.

The Indy, February 1990

Hope

We've netted the land
  with iron tapes
ceaselessly weighted
  Gridded it
with hedges chopped bare
  Contoured it
with lines and numbers

Angled lined hatched
  squared off
Gouged out pits and tunnels
  refilled with filth
Poured our foulness
  in river and sea
Our poison into the air

Yet the hill's haloed
  above quick green
Wind-carved trees stand
  against going sun
We're here and
  something in us
is pure and lasting as landscape.

Anne Born

Swan nesting amongst rubbish by the River Clyde, Glasgow

The Whisper

Around the world the whisper goes,
A gentle, universal breath,
And everything that hears it grows.

At its command the river flows,
A blade of light, a glittering sheath –
Around the world the whisper goes.

What it is saying no one knows
Although it tells of life not death
And everything that hears it grows.

It takes the measure of its foes,
It makes a garland of a wreath –
Around the world the whisper goes.

It fills with hope the wind that blows
Across the desolated heath
And everything that hears it grows.

Above us all, it still bestows
A blessing on what lies beneath.
Around the world the whisper goes
And everything that hears it grows.

John Mole

IS it not easy to conceive the World in your Mind? To think the Heavens fair? The Sun Glorious? The Earth fruitful? The Air Pleasant? the Sea Profitable? And the Giver bountiful? Yet these are the things which it is difficult to retain. For could we always be sensible of their use and value, we should be always delighted with their wealth and glory.

from *Centuries of Meditation* by Thomas Traherne

Just as some stories tell of a time when there was no light and no sun, the following Aborigine story from the north-west of Western Australia relates how darkness first came to the earth.

Daughter sun, mother sun, and all the stars, were diving for waterlily bulbs. Mother sun thought she would take a walk. She collected her walking sticks (the sun's rays) and went out till she came to the cypress pine trees. She tried to go through them but she was jammed between the pines and couldn't get through so she turned back. Daughter sun said she would come. She got her walking sticks (her rays). She was going to the pine trees. She put her walking sticks, the sun's beams, through, and came through, then climbed up. While she was coming up the sky, a rattlesnake saw her. He waited for her in the middle of the pines and when she came closer, the rattlesnake sprang and fought her. As they fought the rattlesnake bit her all over. She hit him back with her walking sticks and she rolled around in pain. She was rolling down low. She stood all her walking sticks up, then she rolled down out of sight, and it was dark.

Elkin Umbagai, Mowanjum

Backlash

My dream is of trees, forests that grew
voices of boys in their swarming boughs,
self-wrenching suddenly free of it all . . .
the money, the whining saws.

My dream is of trees falling on us –
lumbering out of a rootless sky
thunder black, intent as bombs . . .
so slowly we have time for terror.

My dream is of trunks toppling:
absolved righteous kamikazes
falling savage on their suicidal catalysts
the paper men who slew and pulped them.

The artillery of that huge eruption
batters my ears wooden.
And I fall with my kind, their ignorance
blown like waste paper over sand.

Geoffrey Holloway

CHILDREN JOIN IN SYMBOLIC VOYAGE

A group of children are enjoying an amazing trip to the world's biggest remaining wilderness – the frozen continent of Antarctica – in the company of one of the greatest living explorers, Jacques Cousteau.

On the unforgettable expedition is one child from each of the other six continents in the world – Europe, North and South America, Africa, Asia and Australia.

The elderly explorer, who became famous because of his underwater nature films, said he invited the children to join him to make a symbolic point at a time when the future of Antarctica hangs in the balance.

'We are going on behalf of the generations to come – the children of tomorrow,' he said. 'I decided to have them step on this virgin land, as big as the continental United States, and have them realise that it will be their responsibility to either care for it, or exploit it.'

Cousteau wants to win popular support for a French and Australian plan to protect the South Pole and the icy wastes around it, by turning it into a giant nature reserve.

Britain and the United States oppose that plan. They want to allow mining companies to dig up its minerals – thought to be some of the richest underground reserves in the world.

The children were due to arrive in the Antarctic at the weekend, so long as the weather wasn't too rough. They set sail on board Cousteau's own scientific research ship last week from Punta Arenas on the southern tip of Chile in South America.

The European representative is Elise Otzenberger, an 11-year-old schoolgirl from Paris. That's where Jacques Cousteau originally came from, and where most of the other children on the trip go to school.

It won't be all play during the expedition. They'll have lessons on board ship – and watch Cousteau's team of scientists at work.

Early Times, 11th January 1990

Haiku

The greenhouse effect
is coming to earth to burn
so we had better cool it.

Matthew Roughton
The Vyne School

Figures are hard to come by, but Friends of the Earth reckon a conservative average of 200,000 sq kms of rain forest are lost across the globe each year, with South America being the most affected area. According to FoE the Brazilian jungle disappeared at the rate of a football field a second in last year's burning season.

from Green Magazine, January 1990

My Moon

My moon goes everywhere.
My moon is happy because you are sleeping
and dreaming.
My moon is beyond pines and firs.
My moon is blue shadow under almond trees.
My moon has a flair for silence.
My moon plans the wedding day of honey and rain.
My moon loves to pilgrimage,
skimming hill and field
and coming home to me.
Dreaming of my moon,
I slide down her bosom of outstanding scenery,
her belly of whiteness.
My moon is sweet water I wash in.
I am always her last word.

Penelope Shuttle

Bonus

Teacher's just told us
that 30,000 tonnes
of cosmic debris
arrives from outer space
every year.

I'll tell my Mum
to give up dusting.

Patricia Pogson

LUNAR-CY?

THOUSANDS of people have been calling a special telephone number to find out the temperature on the moon!

American Express' New York weather line provides temperatures and forecasts for 600 places around the world – and one place out of this world.

More people have called for the moon's temperatures than anywhere else, except New York City.

In case you're wondering: it's hot on the sunny half of the moon, about 129 degrees Centigrade (264 degrees Fahrenheit), and cold on the dark half, about minus 169 degrees C (-272 degrees F).

Early Times, 11 January 1990

Leisure

What is this life, if, full of care,
We have no time to stand and stare,

No time to stand beneath the boughs
And stare as long as sheep or cows.

No time to see, when woods we pass,
Where squirrels hide their nuts in grass.

No time to see, in broad daylight,
Streams full of stars, like skies at night.

No time to turn at Beauty's glance,
And watch her feet, how they can dance.

No time to wait till her mouth can
Enrich that smile her eyes began.

A poor life this if, full of care,
We have no time to stand and stare.

W H Davies

Activities

Class discussion

Read 'The Mark of the Beast' on page 100. Remembering your earlier discussions on painters and sculptors, suggest ways in which they and other artists might be able to help. Include writers, composers, and choreographers in your discussion.

John Fairfax says of his poem 'Whose Anyway?':

'This poem sets out to say that the earth, and all in, on, and around it, doesn't "belong" to anyone or thing. At most we're all tenants.'

Do you agree? Or have you ever felt a patch of garden, or wood, or land, was 'yours'? Is it 'yours' because you own it, or because you care for it? Discuss what the difference is between a landowner and a gardener.

Group activities

Using reference books, look up the different groupings of stars ('constellations') and plot them on a wall chart. There are many legends about how these constellations were formed: do you know any of them? Share them with the group if you can.
Write your own story, saying how *you* think they came into being: perhaps giants in another galaxy were playing marbles, and dropped a few. Be as outrageous as you like.

Go back over the whole book. Pick two poems that best illustrate what is said in 'The Mark of the Beast' and prepare a performance. Practise reading the poems loudly and clearly. Don't rush! Then perform them to the rest of the class.

Pair activities

Read again the poem 'Spring Clean' by John Mole. Why is the flower taking all the blame? Using this poem as a model, write a poem about:

(a) the sea and a fish

(b) the sky and a bird.

Read Robert Frost's poem 'Fire and Ice'. One of you be fire and one of you be ice. Write alternate stanzas of a poem, each saying why you are more powerful than the other.

Individual writing

Read again the poem 'My Moon' by Penelope Shuttle. We feel very close to the moon because it revolves around us: it's a 'satellite' to our planet.

Other planets are too far away for us to see, but we know what they look like because photographs have been taken from space rockets. Is there any planet you especially like? Find out more about them before you decide on your favourite: use reference books to help you. Look at Venus, Neptune, Jupiter, Saturn, Uranus, Pluto, Mars and Mercury. Then write a poem about your planet.

Read 'Lunar-cy?' on page 106. Then, taking into account the moon temperature, write a 'day' in the life of a moon creature.

Study closely the poem 'Leisure' by W H Davies. Then add your own stanzas to it, trying to keep to the same form. Notice the poet's use of repetition and rhyme.

Read the Aboriginal story 'Daughter Sun, Mother Sun, and all the Stars'. Write stories explaining other natural phenomena, for example, how the following first came to earth: thunder, lightning, earthquake.

Read 'Children Join in Symbolic Voyage' on page 105.

Imagine you were one of the children picked to go to Antarctica. Write the diary entry for your best day.

Extension

Make a final display, publication or performance of all the work done.

For the display, include poems, paintings, sculptures, photographs, posters, information packs, wallcharts and botanical drawings.

Or you could have a public performance of songs, poems, stories and tape recordings. Tickets could be sold to buy flowers, plants or trees for the school gardens.

Your school might also be able to produce a book of your poems, which could then be sold in aid of green charities. (These are listed at the end of this book.) Some of these charities have special membership rates for children: you might like to join. You could also consider setting up a Green Club at the school, with its own magazine. Include poems, drawings, stories, articles, interviews, a crossword, a queries page, and a letters page.

LIST OF USEFUL ADDRESSES

Here are some charities and other organisations which cater specifically for teachers and/or children:

Animal Aid
7 Castle Street
Tonbridge Kent TN9 1BH
Tel: 0732 364546
Teachers' pack including project booklet *Why Animal Rights* available on request. Also Animal Aid Youth Group for 12-18 year olds.

BOBARS
Muncaster Castle
Ravenglass Cumbria
Tel: 0229 717393
The British Owl Breeding & Release Scheme specialises in owl breeding, conservation and study. Tours of the Centre and lecture, *The Owl Man*, offered to schools: send sae for details.

British Trust for Conservation Volunteers
Publicity Department
36 St Mary's Street
Wallingford Oxon OX10 0EU
Tel: 0491 39766
Protects and improves the environment by practical action. Produces series of resource sheets for teachers, called *Lifeclass*. Send sae for information on schools membership.

Children's Tropical Forests UK
The Old Rectory
Church Street
Market Deeping
Peterborough PE6 8DA
Tel: 0778 346859
Aims to raise awareness, taking positive action to show children how they can raise funds and be instrumental in saving the rainforests. Protection projects currently operating in Central America and Thailand. Send A4 sae for details.

Common Ground
45 Shelton Street
London WC2H 9HJ
Tel: 071 379 3109
Forges links between the practice and enjoyment of the arts and the conservation of landscape and nature. Their many publications include *PULP!* newspaper and its educational supplement *SPLINTER*; an anthology of poetry about trees, *Trees Be Company*; and an A1 poster showing how trees work.

Community Service Volunteers
237 Pentonville Road
London N1 9NJ
Tel: 071 278 6601
The advisory service works with teachers to develop community involvement across the curriculum through publishing, training and innovative pilot projects.

Compassion in World Farming
20 Lavant Street
Petersfield
Hants GU32 3EW
Tel: 0730 68863
A schools resources list is available for teachers upon request. There is a youth group, Farm Animal Rangers, and a junior magazine, *Out*.

Council for National Parks
45 Shelton Street
London WC2H 9HJ
Tel: 071 240 3603
Campaigns to protect national parks and promote their quiet enjoyment by everyone. Schools information pack available on retail.

The David Shepherd Conservation Foundation
PO Box 123
Godalming, Surrey GU8 4JS
Tel: 048632 576
Raises funds in support of conservation projects worldwide. Individual and corporate Young Friends membership category. Information resource pack *Our Fragile World* available for schools.

Earthwatch Headquarters
680 Mount Auburn Street
PO Box 403
Watertown
MA 02272-9104
Provides opportunities for outstanding teachers to participate in sponsored field science projects.

Earthwatch Australia
PO Box C360
Clarence Street
Sydney 2000
Australia
As above.

Earthwatch California
861 Via de la Paz
Suite G
Pacific Palisades
CA 90272
As above.

Earthwatch Europe
Belsyre Court
57 Woodstock Road
Oxford OX2 6HU
Tel: 0865 311600
As above

Elefriends
Cherry Tree Cottage
Coldharbour
Dorking
Surrey RH5 6HA
Tel: 0306 713320
Supports anti-poaching and conservation initiatives in the field, and tackles consumer ivory markets around the world. Individual and schools subscriptions available. Children receive information pack, *Trumpet* magazine, poster and merchandise leaflets.

Environmental Investigation Agency
208-209 Upper Street
London N1 1RL
Tel: 071 704 9441
Works for endangered species. Leaflets and posters available on receipt of large sae.

Friends of the Earth
26-28 Underwood Street
London N1 7JQ
Tel: 071 490 1555
FoE has a teachers and schools subscription scheme. Services include annual mailing of educational material, quarterly flagship magazine *Earth Matters*, and discount on all FoE publications.

The Geologists' Association
Burlington House
Piccadilly
London W1V 9AG
Tel: 071 434 9298
Has established a Code for Geological Field Work, and will be working with Watch on future projects (*Rock Watch*). Their motto: *Rocks need friends.*

Greenpeace UK
Canonbury Villas
London N1 2PN
Tel: 071 354 5100

Briefings available on a number of environmental subjects for Primary and Secondary Schools. Write for details.

International Centre for Conservation Education
Greenfield House
Guiting Power
Cheltenham Glos GL54 5TZ
Tel: 0451 850549
Details of audio-visual material and training courses available to teachers on request. Send A5 sae for catalogue.

International Council for Bird Preservation
32 Cambridge Road
Girton Cambridge CB3 0PJ
Tel: 0223 277318
Works to save threatened birds and their habitats throughout the world. Write to the Information Officer for details of the organisation, its campaigns and how to help.

League Against Cruel Sports
83-87 Union Street
London SE1 1SG
Tel: 071 407 0979
Pleased to supply schools pack to teachers on all aspects of cruel sports. Send large sae.

Lifewatch
London Zoo
Regents Park
London NW1 4RY
Tel: 071 722 3333
Lifewatch's work with animals extends to field conservation projects in Africa and Asia. Membership provides special events, magazines and entry privileges.

London Ecology Centre
45 Shelton Street
London WC2H 9HJ
Tel: 071 379 4324
Offers information service, referring people to specialist organisations. Please enclose sae with enquiries.

Lynx
PO Box 300
Nottingham NG1 5HN
Tel: 0602 413052
Send sae for school pack containing information about Lynx and its campaign against the fur trade.

Marine Conservation Society
9 Gloucester Road
Ross-on-Wye
Herefordshire HR9 5BU
Tel: 0989 66017
Teachers information pack, sales catalogue and fact sheets suitable for all ages available on receipt of sae.

National Society for Clean Air
136 North Street
Brighton BN1 1RG
Tel: 0273 26313
Information packs and leaflets on air pollution available on request.

The Rain Forest Trust
QA Box 5
Ansculf House
Dudley
West Midlands DY2 8PE
Tel: 0384 288229
Send sae for leaflets and brochures.

Royal Society for the Protection of Birds
Education Dept
The Lodge
Sandy
Bedfordshire SG19 2DL
Tel: 0767 680551
Teaching resources pack available to teachers on request. See also The Young Ornithologists' Club.

The Soil Association
86-88 Colston Street
Bristol
Avon BS1 5BB
Tel: 0272 290661
Educational material available to teachers. Recent developments include slide set, colourful poster and information sheets. Please send large sae with enquiries.

Transport 2000
Walkden House
10 Melton Street
London NW1 2EJ
Tel: 071 388 8386
Campaigns for environmental transport policy. Send large sae for fact packs.

Watch
(Junior branch of The Royal Society for Nature Conservation)
The Green
Witham Park
Lincoln LN5 7JR
Tel: 0522 44400
Send sae for information on educational projects packs: many topics from acid rain to bumblebees.

Whales and Dolphins Conservation Society

19A James Street West
Bath Avon BA1 2BT
Tel: 0225 334511
Educational full colour bulletin available free to teachers: A4 sae appreciated. Membership benefits include *Sonar* magazine and newsletters. Books, tapes, videos and international whale bulletins available on retail.

The Woodland Trust

Autumn Park
Dysart Road
Grantham
Lincs NG31 6LL
Tel: 0476 74297
Educational pack available to teachers on request. Please send 9" x 14" sae.

World Society for the Protection of Animals

1A Park Place
Lawn Lane
Vauxhall
London SW8
Tel: 071 793 0540
Range of information available to teachers on most international animal welfare and conservation issues. Send large sae.

WWF UK

Education Dept
Panda House
Weyside Park
Godalming
Surrey GU7 1XR
Tel: 0483 426444
WWF (World Wide Fund for Nature) Education Department has published over 100 books, posters, teaching packs and cassettes for schools to cater for all ages and subjects. Discount offered under special teacher membership scheme.

The Young Ornithologists' Club

RSPB
The Lodge
Sandy
Bedfordshire SG19 2DL
Tel: 0767 680551
The Young Ornithologists' Club, junior membership of the RSPB, is the national club for young people interested in birds and wildlife.

Young People's Trust for the Environment and Nature Conservation

95 Woodbridge Road
Guildford
Surrey GU1 4PY
Tel: 0483 39600
Offers comprehensive information service on wildlife and environmental matters, one-day field trips, residential field courses and a school lecture service. Please enclose large sae with enquiries.

Zoocheck

Cherry Tree Cottage
Coldharbour
Dorking
Surrey RH5 6HA
Tel: 0306 712091
Project information available on request: sae appreciated. Also educational handbook available on retail to teachers.

Acknowledgements

The author would like to thank David Orme for his invaluable help and advice.

The author would also like to thank Liz Paren and Gill Stacey, Editorial Consultants, for their equally invaluable work.

The author wishes to thank the following schools for permission to use poems written by pupils while the author was Writer in Residence or visiting poet: Chawton C E (Controlled) Primary School, Alton; Heathfield School, Taunton; Oakridge Junior School, Basingstoke; Shaw House School, Newbury and Berkshire Information Technology Team, Wokingham; The Vyne School, Basingstoke; Westwood St Thomas' School, Salisbury.

The author and publishers wish to thank the following for copyright poems written specially for this book:

Joan Aiken for 'New Town' and 'Thrush'
Leo Aylen for 'Greedy Green River'
Anne Born for 'Hope'
Debjani Chatterjee for 'Jumbo Proverb Haiku' and 'Please Save the Porcupine'
Wendy Cope for 'Composer'
John Cotton for 'Ice'
Matthew Cousens for 'Haiku'
Matthew Day for 'Leaving'
Peter Dixon for 'Boxer's Lake' and 'Sky High Sailor'
Carol Ann Duffy for 'English Summer'
Elizabeth Dunne for 'Haiku'
Edna Eglinton for 'Riverside Cabaret'
Clare Emery for 'Haiku'
Gavin Ewart for 'Going to Guyana'
John Fairfax for extract from *Pictures in the Seed* and 'Whose Anyway?'
Michael Fairfax for interview with the author
Nigel Forde for 'A Quiet Day' and 'From the Hill'
Pamela Gillilan for 'Lion'
Geoffrey Holloway for 'Backlash' and 'Chart Topper'
Hannah Kirby for 'Haiku'
Harry Laing for 'Croft-Dhu, Inverness-shire'
Medbh McGuckian for 'The Hunter'
Norman MacCaig for 'Dipper'

Wes Magee for 'The Buttercup Experiment' and 'The Old Tree Stump'
Sally Anne Marsh for 'The Puddle'
Lee Matthews for 'The Living Planet'
Trevor Millum for 'Meadow Avenue' and 'No One Wants to be a Handbag'
John Mole for 'Spring Clean' and 'The Whisper'
Judith Nicholls for 'Sealsong'
David Orme for 'Beside the Seaside' and 'Fireweed in the Park'
Fiona Pearson for 'What Rain Does'
Patricia Pogson for 'Bonus' and 'May Evening'
Sheenagh Pugh for 'Quetzals Only Come Once'
Matthew Roughton for two Haikus
Kellie Ruffles for 'Haiku'
Adrian Ryder for 'Haiku'
Lawrence Sail for 'That Flower'
Penelope Shuttle for 'My Moon'
Kim Stock for 'There's Thunder in the Air'
Matthew Sweeney for 'Christopher' and 'Jan'
Adam Thorpe for 'The Sea Moaning'
Edward Wall for 'The Teabag'
Celia Ward for interview with the author
Blossom Wyson for 'Wood'
James Younger for 'Haiku'

The publishers also wish to thank Sue Stewart for 'Five Haiku', 'Greater Spotted' and 'Mr Middleton Says'.

The author and publishers wish to thank the following who have kindly given permission for the use of copyright material.

Joan Aiken, for an extract from 'A Leaf in the Shape of a Key' from *The Last Slice of Rainbow*, Jonathan Cape,1985. Copyright © Joan Aiken; Anvil Press Poetry Ltd., for 'Two Haiku' by E. A. Markham from *Living in Disguise*, 1986; Curtis Brown Ltd., on behalf of the author for 'Song of the Open Road' by Ogden Nash, *New Yorker*. Copyright © 1932 by Ogden Nash; Early Times, newspaper for young people, for extracts from various issues; Green Magazine Co. Ltd., for extract from *Green Magazine*, January 1990; William Heinemann Ltd., for an extract from *The Little Prince* written by A. de Saint Exupéry, trans. by Katherine Woods, 1945 Houghton Mifflin Company, for an extract from *A Wizard of Earthsea* by Ursula K. Le Guin. Copyright © 1968 by The Intert-Vivos Trust for the Le Guin Children; Macmillan Publishing Company, for 'Song of the Animal World' from *The Unwritten Song*, Vol. 1 ed. and trans. Willard R. Trask. Copyright © 1966 by Willard R. Trask; Macmillan, London and Basingstoke, and Mrs Hodgson for 'Stupidity Street' from *Poems* by Ralph Hodgson; Methuen Childrens Books, for an extract from 'Owls are Night Birds' by Berlie Doherty in *Streets Ahead* by Valerie Bierman; Malcolm Miles, for an extract from *Resurgence*, No. 131, Nov-Dec., 1988; John Moat, for 'Four Quarters' and adapted story 'The Tree Man' from *The Man Who Planted Trees* by Jean Giono. Copyright © 1985 Chelsea Green Publishing Co.; Judith Nicholls for 'Bamboozled' from forthcoming collection; Brian Patten, for 'It's Poisoning Down' from *Thawing Frozen Frogs*, Viking, 1990; Pantheon Books, a division of Random House, Inc., for 'World', 'Full Moon' and 'Ceremony' from *Greek Lyric Poetry*, trans. Willis Barnstone, Schocken Books. Copyright © 1962, 1967 by Willis Barnstone; Penguin Books Ltd., for extracts from *The Narrow road to the Deep North and Other Travel Sketches* by Bashō, trans. Nobuyuki Yuasa, Penguin Classics, Copyright © 1966 Nobuyuki Yuasa, and *Island of the Blue Dolphins* by Scott O'Dell, Kestrel Books, 1961. Copyright © 1960 Scott O'Dell; and 'The Tree-planter Laughs at Himself' by Yuan Mei from *The Penguin Book of Chinese Verse*, trans. Robert Kotewall and Norman L. Smith, Penguin Books, Copyright © 1962 N. L. Smith and R. H. Kotewell; Jonathon Porritt for extract from his Schumacher Lecture, 1988; Random Century Group, on behalf of the Estate of W. H. Davies for 'Leisure' from *The Complete Poems of W. H. Davies*; 'Airy Hall Iconography' from *Airy Hall* by Fred D'Aguiar, Chatto & Windus, 1989, and 'Mama Dot's Treatise' from *Mama Dot* by Fred D'Aguiar, Chatto & Windus; on behalf of the Estate of Robert Frost for 'Fire and Ice' from *The Poetry of Robert Frost,* ed. Edward Connery Lathem, Jonathan Cape; Roland Robinson, for extract by Eustan Williams from *The Man Who Sold His Dreaming* by Roland Robinson; Olive Senior, for 'Birdshooting Season' from *Talking of Trees*, Calabash, Kingston. Copyright © 1985 Olive Senior; Sidgwick & Jackson Ltd., for 'The Last Forest' from *Return to Zululand* by Leo Aylen; Solo Syndication and Literary Agency Ltd., for extract from *Daily Mail*, 3. 1. 90; Weldon Publishing, for extract from *Australian Dreaming* by Jennifer Isaacs, Lansdowne Press; Young Newspaper Publishing Ltd., for 'Mark of the Beast', *The Indy*, No. 19, 1. 2. 90.

Every effort has been made to trace all the copyright holders but if any have been inadvertently overlooked the publishers will be pleased to make the necessary arrangement at the first opportunity.

The publishers would like to thank the following for permission to reproduce copyright photographs:

Photographers

Environmental Picture Library

Graham Burns p101
Pilly Cowell p88
Martin Levy p104
V Miles p47
P Sutherland p4

ICCE Services Ltd

Malcolm Boulton p48
Andy Purcell p28

Network Photographers

Fay Godwin p13

Michael Fairfax p44
Peter Randall-Page p45
John Woodrow p20

Illustrators

Linda Combi p15, p31, p33, p38, p69, p70, p83, p86, p103
Val Grace section openings and p50, p58, p66, p84, p98, p117
Jonathan Fairfax p23
Truda Lane p76, p93, p107
Dave Parker p6, p8, p24, p26, p53, p64, p79, p80, p82, p98
Carole Smethurst p3, p16, p62

Haiku

Frogs hop up and down.
I bet they could jump from here
to Australia.

Kellie Ruffles
Oakridge Junior School